Phillida Sawbridge has been the director of the London-based Post-Adoption Centre since it opened in 1986. She has specialised in adoption work since 1967 and written and lectured widely on the subject.

John Triseliotis is Professor of Social Work at Edinburgh University. He has carried out research, taught and lectured in many countries on issues concerned with adoption and foster care. He is the author and co-author of several books on adoption issues, from *In search of origins* in 1973 (Routledge & Kegan Paul) to *Parting with a child for adoption* in 1991 (with Bouchier P and Lambert L, BAAF).

Doreen Ward became actively involved in adoption issues after attending the first birth mothers group run by the Post-Adoption Centre in 1987. She believes that it is important to speak out on behalf of the many women who are still the hidden members of the adoption story. She is now a co-ordinator of the Natural Parents' Support Group and is committed to an improvement of pre- and post-adoption services for birth parents.

Contents

This book is dedicated to my parents

Audrey Mullender

Foreword

Adoption has been around for as long as humans, or animals for that matter, have organised themselves socially into family groups. Throughout this time we have tended to learn more about those cases when it was less than successful – Oedipus and Moses being but two well-known examples from literature and history. Yet adoption has always served a purpose for at least some of those – birth parents, adopters and children – who make up the 'adoption triad'. The purpose, and the form taken, has however varied at different times and in different cultures. The types of adoption which most of us who are currently working in this field have grown up with, and which was legislated for in 1926, is the formally organised, closed model which, in its 'purest' form, totally severs one set of relationships and replaces them with another set. I say most of us, because in our increasingly multi-cultural society, growing numbers of adoption workers are familiar with a different and more open model which is the norm in many (perhaps most) cultures other than the European/North American one.

The total severance model encouraged by the 1926 Act appeared equally functional for all three parts of the adoption triad (or all four, in that the State may also have an interest in the effective functioning of the institution of adoption). Unmarried parents saw in it a way of escaping a life tainted by the stigma of illegitimacy both for themselves and their own families, and for the child. The extent to which it was used over the next 30 years confirms its perceived value as a 'remedy' for the 'mistake' of an unwanted pregnancy. The state and society encouraged the practice. The number of adoption agencies multiplied, in order to help children escape from a life which was expected to be marked by stigma, poverty and other deprivations, and often was. Adoption offered a way of not punishing the child, whilst avoiding the need to help single parents and the appearance of condoning extra-marital sexual relationships. Potential adopters, who at that time were mainly married couples unable to have a family by birth, gained the family they desperately wanted in a way which was officially sanctioned by society. Secrecy appeared to be in everyone's interests. The dominant ideologies were of rescue for the child and, for the adults, forgetting past traumas (of separation, loss, family conflict and infertility) and making a fresh start. Many parents and children tried to convince themselves that adoptive families were exactly the same as families created by birth.

But time moved on. British society became more flexible in its approach to family life, and the post-war welfare state offered more support for the disadvantaged, including single parents. They were the first group to decide that the closed, secret, new-start model of adoption no longer met their needs. They withdrew from it, and this, together with improved methods of birth control and the increasing availability of abortion, caused the number of babies placed for adoption to drop in the dramatic way with which we are now so familiar. This process was accelerated, and has been reinforced, by an increasing awareness amongst professionals and society at large (especially through some moving television documentaries) that the 'fresh start' for the parent giving up a baby for adoption did not always materialise. For an unknown proportion the pain of separation and the trauma of loss never totally went away. An unknown proportion of adoptive parents (some of whom wrote influential research studies, cited in this volume), and adopted teenagers and adults also found that the effects of family creation by adoption, and the events which preceded it, lasted a lifetime. I say 'unknown' because the secrecy surrounding adoption has made it very difficult to undertake research in order to find out not just if the adoption was 'successful' in that it did not break down, but whether the 'fresh start/heal the wounds' hopes of many were realised. Any doubts about the appropriateness of the closed model for babies placed at the birth parents' request were strengthened when the fresh-start approach was used with older children placed against their parents' wishes.

The beginning of the end of this comparatively short-lived experiment of totally closed adoption was the clause in the 1975 Children Act allowing adopted children access to their birth records. Indeed, since they always had this right in Scotland it can be said that the totally closed model was never fully introduced there. The papers in this fascinating and informative volume chart the history of increasing openness in social work and adoptive parenting *practice* in Britain (and New Zealand), through to the point at which the inter-departmental group considering the reform of adoption law has placed it on the agenda of *legal* reformers. This timely collection of papers will undoubtedly have its part to play in the debate leading up to a new Adoption Act for the 1990s and beyond.

June Thoburn
Social Work Development Unit
University of East Anglia, Norwich

Introduction

We make no apology for opening this publication with the statement that we believe it constitutes an important collection of material on the crucial and topical subject of open adoption. Included here are sound academic and professional papers by people with many years' specialist experience in the field of adoption, gained in voluntary and local authority adoption agencies, at the Post-Adoption Centre and in university departments. Importantly, however, in addition to a scholarly overview of the field and reports from research studies and from practice experience in Britain and New Zealand, the book's contents have been contributed directly by members of the adoption triad. The authors include birth mothers, an adoptive parent, an adopted person, and the child of an adopted person, though not all are identified as such in the text. One group still missing here is birth fathers. Perhaps they will be the next group whose views will belatedly influence the agenda for change.

The main overseas country represented is New Zealand and, again, we make no apology for this. It is by now well recognised that New Zealand has made significant advances in relation to openness from which we may have much to learn but, until now, relatively little material on these experiences has been published in this country. A note of caution in relation to the pace and extent of possible changes may be evident from some of the home-based British authors which is not shared by those writing about the New Zealand situation. Perhaps the confidence of these latter will prove to be infectious as we read and learn more about this subject. Both nations are put into a more global context in the opening paper by Professor John Triseliotis. In so doing, he presents some major questions to be answered as we begin the important process of consultation and review of adoption law in England and Wales.

We lead, then, with a scholarly overview by John Triseliotis drawing on experiences from other parts of the world where openness is better known than here. He examines the impetus and rationale for change, as well as questions which must be resolved in considering how best a more open system might be managed. In defining the terms of the debate, Triseliotis reveals some muddled thinking which we cannot afford if we are serious about making a reality of increased openness.

The following section, on the experience of actual open placements, begins with Joan Fratter's interesting research findings on the openness which does already successfully exist in this country. After this come Murray Ryburn's reflections, based largely on open placements in New Zealand but taking into account also his involvement here with, for example, the added complications of contested adoptions. Both papers concentrate largely on the point of view of adoptive parents. This is because, as Ryburn states, the advantages of openness to them have received least attention up to now. Certainly, British practitioners appear to fear that adopters will feel threatened by openness, that they will not come forward to adopt without the protection of secrecy, and that they will prove generally unable to cope with open placements. None of the contributions in this collection bears this out. Perhaps we can begin to expect from adopters what we have long taken for granted in many long-term foster parents – that they can make room in their lives for a birth family who still mean a lot to their child and who may have much to give, even when it is fully acknowledged that they will never again take on the main caring role. Michael Mallows' paper poses the challenge that transracial placements are the most open of all, and that listening to those whose formative years are spent in them raises the question of how far we are all prepared to engage with the racism endemic in our society. My own paper returns to the New Zealand context to examine the growing spread of openness there, as manifested by the opening up of placements which were previously closed, before the adopted person reaches adulthood.

The section of this book which presents the perspective of birth mothers can be regarded, perhaps, as its backbone, so crucial is it to the whole shift of emphasis in adoption towards openness. As we begin to hear the voice of birth mothers, we realise the damage which was done by the old, closed model of secrecy and why things have to change. This may shake the system as profoundly as did John Triseliotis's interviews with young adults wanting access to their birth records in the early 1970s. Adoption may, to many, have seemed cosy and uncontroversial but at what cost? We are privileged to include a first-hand insight into just what the costs were for two birth mothers, as well as for those women who have benefited from the pioneering work of the Post-Adoption Centre, recorded here by Phillida Sawbridge.

Our closing section is concerned with the experience from the adult end of the spectrum, again in New Zealand. Greater openness is reflected there, first in the fact that birth parents have been accorded rights of access to records, and second in the far higher ratio of adopted people who have sought reunions than has happened here. I have set the scene by explaining the workings of the system and the key differences from England and Wales. My paper is followed by a summary of an important new research study by Dr Jeff Field of Auckland University. He illuminates the major difference it makes to birth mothers to have news of and, where desired, a reunion with the person they have not seen since placement for adoption in babyhood. Thus Field echoes, from a research base, the crucial importance of information and contact to birth mothers which others, writing from direct and practice experience, have recorded in earlier chapters. If we are already aware of their meaning, too, to adopted people and if further papers in this collection have answered fears about adopters' views, what obstacles remain to a further spread of openness in this country?

Keith Griffith, writing for the first time in Britain, then picks up the theme of the results of access to records, both for adopted people and their birth parents, as well as the broader lessons these represent. An adopted person himself and a Methodist minister, Keith Griffith was awarded the MBE for his work in spearheading the movement for adoption law reform in New Zealand. He is becoming increasingly recognised in Canada and the USA as someone who can provide the clarity of thought and wealth of experience needed when change is contemplated.

At this significant point in the history of adoption in our own country, it is to be hoped that his and the other contributions included here will provide us with much food for thought. Bon appetit!

Audrey Mullender
Centre for Applied Social Studies
University of Durham

THE EXPERIENCE OF OPEN PLACEMENTS

1 Open adoption

John Triseliotis

There is no doubting the upsurge of interest in open adoption when it also features prominently in the government discussion paper 'The nature and effect of adoption,[1] published in 1990. The paper offers a number of alternative options concerning the transfer of relationships from birth to adoptive family. This chapter discusses the evidence available and some of the advantages and disadvantages of different types of open adoption.

The impetus for change

Interest in open adoption has come about through two main routes. First, studies in the 1960s (by McWhinnie[2]) and early 1970s (by Triseliotis[3]) demonstrated the impact that secrecy surrounding adoption had on the lives of adopted people. Triseliotis' study referred to the reluctance of many adoptive parents to tell children they were adopted, their avoidance of the topic of adoption after the child had been told and their reluctance to share background information or the circumstances of the adoption with the child. As a result some adopted people came to mistrust their adoptive parents and were critical of the secrecy which made them feel embarrassed or 'second class' because they were adopted. The lack of information about their birth parents and about their genealogy made them feel incomplete. The study contributed to changes in the legal systems of a number of countries, including England and Wales, which have made it possible for adopted people to obtain access to their birth records. This also enabled adopted people to pursue the possibility of establishing contact with one or both birth parents, most often the mother. This and subsequent studies were also to confirm that, irrespective of the search for a birth parent, in the adopted person's mind their 'real' parents remained the people who brought them up and not those who gave birth to them.

Adopted people have increasingly been asking for more openness in adoption and a move away from the undue secrecy that has

17

surrounded it. Indeed, a recent study by Craig[4] has found much greater openness and significantly improved communication existing between adoptive parents and their adopted children, compared to that of the past. Craig interviewed a group of adoptive parents and their adopted children, separately, to contrast their respective views on openness. The adoptive parents had been well prepared by the placing agency in the early 1970s on how to tell their children about their adoption and had also been given written information on the birth parents to pass on. The picture that emerges from this study is of infinitely more openness than before and almost none of the children involved said that secrecy and evasiveness went with adoption.

Another set of recent studies in America,[5] Australia[6] and Scotland[7] have begun to identify the long-term adverse psychological effects of relinquishment on birth mothers. Millen and Roll[8] have linked relinquishment to pathological mourning and related this enduring anguish to the seven grief reactions identified by Parkes,[9] namely: realisation, alarm, searching, anger and guilt, loss of self, identification and pathological variants. Other characteristics displayed by mothers studied by Millen and Roll included unresolved anger, searching in waking life or in dreams, and a sense of incompleteness. The prolonged effects of relinquishment were also established by Deykin et al.[10]

Though all these studies were biased in one way or another, in that they failed to follow up representative samples, nevertheless the message that comes across is of long and lasting distress for many of these mothers. Some of the studies suggested that counselling to facilitate grief work, both at the time of adoption and later, would have been appropriate. A high proportion of the mothers in the studies quoted were now seeking to establish contact with the child they had surrendered or were asking for news about them. It is assumed that open adoption should make relinquishment feel easier for birth parents, helping to reduce the negative psychological impacts mentioned above.

The second impetus for change in Britain, and possibly the one that set off the debate, has been a result of developments in adoption practice over the last 15 years or so. The practice of terminating parental contact or the 'clean break' approach followed by some agencies, especially when placing older children, has been critically *(handwritten margin notes: "1) child brought up in secrecy 2) older child adopted, both affected by break")*

examined elsewhere[11] and its flaws identified. Great distress has been caused to some children and their parents as a result of this approach, and the importance of maintaining meaningful links in such adoptions has been stressed. This has also been reinforced by Fratter's recent study,[12] part of which is summarised elsewhere in this book.

The secrecy built into adoption practice and adoption legislation is a product of the last 70 years. Although there was no legislation regarding adoption practice in the UK until 1926, a form of open *de facto* adoption existed, not dissimilar to that still to be found in some of the Pacific Islands and in African countries. Adoption in these countries, however, is largely confined to the children of relatives.

The secrecy which was introduced, particularly into English adoption legislation and into adoption practice, was seen as necessary to protect mothers of non-marital children, and the children themselves, from excessive stigma. It was also felt that childless couples could avoid the equally oppressive taint of infertility as a result of this secrecy. Furthermore, at a time when there were more children requiring new families than applicants, the assurance of secrecy was intended to encourage more would-be adopters to come forward. Adopters would then be able to bring up the children without the fear of interference from the birth parent(s). It is not surprising that all these well-intended measures and practices contributed to the development of widespread secrecy concerning adoption, including the reluctance of adoptive parents to tell the child about the adoption and their failure to acknowledge, in Kirk's words,[13] 'the difference' between adoptive and biological parenthood.

In examining the concept of open adoption, it is useful to view it from the perspectives of the three protagonists and to try to identify how their interests are promoted or impeded. In the absence of studies in all the areas under discussion, only tentative conclusions can be drawn. Before that, though, it is important to clarify the terms used in describing open adoption.

Getting the terms right
Terms such as 'semi-open' adoption, 'open' adoption and 'adoption with contact' are often used interchangeably, and sometimes misleadingly. The term 'adoption with contact' is unique to Britain and possibly North America where, during the last couple of decades, a

19

determined effort has been made to find adoptive and sometimes permanent foster families for children with special needs. In the process, important links between some children and their parents, grand-parents and other relatives have been, as was pointed out earlier, unwisely severed. Adoption with contact preserves these meaningful links with members of the birth family, whilst also providing stability and continuity of care in these children's lives. The degree of contact obviously depends upon the child's needs.

'Open adoption' refers mostly to the adoption of infants, with the birth parent being actively involved in hearing about and choosing from a number of would-be adopters. There are a number of variations on this procedure, depending on the agency and the wishes and preferences of the parties involved. Most of our current knowledge in open adoption comes from New Zealand, where it has been practised for at least a decade, and more recently from the USA, particularly from those states which do not prohibit third party or independent adoptions. In New Zealand, the birth parent selects adopters from written profiles, which they have often prepared themselves, and, after the birth, meets the couple she has chosen, whilst some private agencies in the USA introduce the expectant birth mother to several couples from whom she then makes her choice. This will be explored further in a later section of this paper.

The term 'semi-open' adoption describes what is possibly a widespread practice among adoption agencies nowadays. This involves the agency in providing full, but non-identifying, information to the birth parent(s) and would-be adopters about each other. Birth parents may also have a role in choosing the couple to bring up their child but without meeting them in person. A recent example of this practice is described by Fish and Speirs[14] arising from their work experiences with an adoption agency based in Montreal, Canada. In this case, the agency narrows down the number of would-be adopters to three, a profile is developed on each one of them, and the birth parent is asked to select two of the couples. A preferred couple is selected and, in the event that they are not available, an alternative one. No face-to-face meetings are arranged.

The agency does the screening and the birth parent has 'controlled' choice. A variation on the above seems relatively widespread in British baby placements now and involves one meeting after the birth but no exchange of surnames or addresses.

20

One question currently being asked is whether agencies should now be passing the possible decision of 'rejecting' applicants on to the biological parent(s). In Britain, both parties are also prepared for the possibility that, when the child reaches his or her late teens, they may wish to establish contact with a birth parent. Equally, a birth parent may wish to do the same although the possibilities for this are currently very restricted. Most adoption agencies also encourage both parties to up-date the agency about themselves and, in the case of the adopters, about the child's progress. Such non-identifying information may be passed, on request, to each of the parties involved.

The rationale for open adoption and adoption with contact

Greater, or indeed full, openness is promoted on the grounds that it is better for all the parties involved, particularly for the child and then for the birth parent(s). When it comes to the adopting couple the picture that emerges from the theoretical and research literature is so far less certain and more ambiguous.

a) The children

Open adoption, it is believed, will contribute to increased feelings of well-being among adopted people and generally enhance their identity, self-image and self-concept. As a result, it should also contribute to a significant reduction in the behavioural and emotional difficulties found in studies of adopted people which are attributed to the secrecy surrounding adoption. Though such studies present contradictory findings concerning the presence of 'disturbed' behaviour among adopted people compared to the rest of the population, nevertheless, where difficulties have been identified, these frequently (though not always) focus on issues of identity and/or the experience of being adopted. Secrecy, as epitomised by evasiveness or the absence of physical images of the birth parents, is only one ingredient that may spoil the formation of positive identity; the importance of parenting quality and of community attitudes and perceptions should not be underestimated. Our studies suggest that open communication about adoption is only one important variable contributing to the formation of a positive personal and social identity.

Why should greater openness lead to a more certain and secure sense of self? First, by meeting the biological parent(s), the adoptive parents obtain direct information about them, their interests,

21

background, and so on, to pass on to the child, as well as recognising the possibility of ongoing contact. They should also find it easier to acknowledge that adoption is different from biological parenthood. The possibility of continued or of periodic contact should enable the child to have visual images of the birth parent(s) and to be in a position to ask questions about them, including why he or she was given up for adoption. The child's developing personality will be based from the start on the concept of two sets of families – a birth family and a psychological family. This is an additional developmental task that non-adopted children do not have to cope with, except perhaps children in re-constituted families and those born through assisted reproduction. With open adoption there will be no sudden revelations and no possibility for evasiveness or distortion; perhaps more important, the feelings of rejection that appear endemic in adoption may be eliminated or reduced.[15] (Though not the subject of this paper, one might strongly argue that if we have open adoption then why not also open assisted reproduction?)

The arguments outlined above are powerful and seem valid, but sufficient empirical evidence to support them is still lacking. A New Zealand study[16] followed up adoptive families in the first years after the adoption, but long-term follow-up studies, including interviews with the children, are still to come. The main argument put forward against open adoption is that children will be unable to attach themselves to the psychological parents when they also maintain contact or links with a non-custodial birth parent and/or relatives. Furthermore, that the maintenance of such links will confuse the child who may come to feel that he or she belongs to neither family. Of adoptive parents who met birth parents in Dominick's study, however, almost half said that the meeting helped them to build a relationship with the child and the rest said that the meeting did not hinder their relationship with the child.

Goldstein et al[17] have argued, from a clinical rather than an empirical base, for the cessation of contact between a child and his or her birth parents once the child is with new carers, on the grounds that otherwise, the child would fail to bond with them. They go on to make similar claims about children of divorce, arguing that the growth of bonding and attachment of the child to a step-parent would be impeded by continued contact with a non-custodial parent. Though the evidence from studies of children living in households

22

involving a step-parent and a custodial parent are somewhat imprecise, what evidence emerges suggests that children have no difficulty in relating positively both to their biological parents and to a step-parent. Problems usually arise when the adults involved in the situation handle access and visits in an acrimonious and hostile way. As a result, these children's loyalties can be stretched, placing them sometimes in an impossible position.

The studies also suggest that, unlike young children, adolescents seem to find it harder to relate to a step-father when they already have a good relationship with a non-custodial father.[18] These writers go on to add that the younger the children, the less difficulty they find in admitting a step-parent or step-sibling into their lives. Furstenberg[19] also found that children could be just as attached to a step-father when they continued to see the biological, non-custodial father on a regular basis. The writer goes on to add, though, that the children appeared to have more difficulty in simultaneously handling relationships with two mothers. From a review of the relevant research literature, Schaffer[20] observes that 'children adjust better to the step-family if they have a continuing relationship'. This view is also supported by recent adoption studies where a child had maintained links with a member of the biological family.[21]

Possibly the most cogent lesson we can take from re-constituted families with access by a non-custodial parent is that, for access to work and to be beneficial to the child, it depends on how the adults involved handle visits, relationships, and so on. In other words – and this will be true also in situations of continued contact in adoption – we must ask how far, given the unpredictability of human behaviour, can adults co-operate without rancour or conflict? For example, one of the main sources of conflict in adoption with contact as practised in some Pacific Islands, is the perceived 'interference' of the natural family.[22]

Fox[23] reports that Kibbutzim children, too, have no difficulty in relating to more than one parental figure at the same time and that the quality of the relationship with the mother is in no way affected by the fact that she is not the only, and in certain respects not the principal, caretaker. Based on his studies of young children, Schaffer[24] maintains that even young children are capable of differentiating between carers and of attaching themselves to more than one set of carers at the same time. He goes on to add that 'the fear that the relationship is in some way going to be "diluted" by the simultaneous existence of other relationships is quite unjustified, a child's attachment is not some limited quantity that has to be divided up amongst people ... moreover, it has also become apparent that children are able to sort out the differing roles of people at much earlier ages than they had been given credit for'. Foster care studies also demonstrate the capacity of children to relate to both birth family figures and to foster carers. Difficulties, though, do arise and are again related to how the parents and foster carers manage the contact. It could be surmised that open adoption, unlike divorce and foster care, should work better because it is not based on an adversarial approach. In addition, the birth parent will have played a big part in the arrangement, in contrast to the scenario that often surrounds divorce or foster care.

When it comes to older children who are adopted, the evidence does not support the 'clean break' approach followed by many agencies. Maintaining links where the child previously had a meaningful relationship with a birth parent or relative seems to help the former to settle in his or her new family.[25] In their study of adoption allowances, Hill and his colleagues[26] came across a number of very distressed children who were lamenting the severance of links between themselves and a parent. Other children, who had no previous meaningful attachments, resisted attempts by parent(s) to establish contact. Practice in this respect has not been very responsive to children's needs and the wishes, especially of older children, were often not sought. Neglecting to establish the wishes and preferences of older children jeopardises the stability of a new placement.

In matters of access, the courts have been reaching inconsistent decisions. Whilst most court decisions during the last 20 or so years have gone against the notion of adoption with contact, a few have provided for this because they were satisfied that it was in the best interests of the child. More often, though, the courts have substituted foster care for adoption, in order not to deprive a parent of continuing contact. This approach has included cases where the parent had made it clear that he or she had no intention of having the child back. In such cases, the best interests of the child for security, continuity of care and a family base in life could have been better served by an adoption order with a condition of contact. (For a more detailed discussion of judicial decisions, see Triseliotis, 1991.[27])

24

Bearing in mind the acrimony and rancour that often surrounds access situations in divorce cases, it might seem irresponsible to introduce a similar approach in adoption. Yet it seems the only way to safeguard an existing link of importance to the child. In baby adoptions, there is a lot to be said for leaving ongoing contact to be based on mutual preferences rather than on compulsion and through court regulation. As a starting point, we will need to develop more experience of the working of open adoption before any such step is considered.

b) The birth parent

Studies based on interviews with birth mothers who relinquished children some ten, 20 or 30 years ago, tend to show their continuing distress, pain and anguish arising from the relinquishment decision.[28] Because of problems of access and sampling, all these studies are biased overwhelmingly towards birth mothers who have been actively seeking information or to establish contact with the surrendered child. Unexpectedly perhaps, even amongst these mothers, their reactions are far from uniform, as is their distress. Little is known about the views, perspective or psychological state of those mothers who are not seeking reunions. Winkler and Keppel,[29] on the basis of their study carried out in Western Australia, argue for better counselling and support services at the relinquishing stage to help the mothers come to terms with their decision, thus preventing continuing distress and depression. Bouchier's Scottish study[30] did not fully support these findings but the amount of lingering distress was considerable.

The studies referred to above assert that these mothers seem not to have come to terms with their decision, are continuing to mourn the child, and are beset by guilt and remorse. As a result, they see the contact as an opportunity to tell the child why they had to give him or her up, to explain their social and personal circumstances at the time that necessitated this, and to ask for a sort of forgiveness. Pannor and Baran[31] have no doubt that open adoption would make it easier for birth parents to cope with their feelings of loss and mourning, and to know also that their child is well. A number of mothers, like some adopted people seeking contact, harbour the hope of a continuing relationship, but this is not always the main impetus for the quest. Above all, what they seem to be after is a kind of reconciliation with

25

the child or the knowledge that the child understands and forgives. In return, the knowledge by the child that he or she was wanted may help to assuage some of the feelings of rejection which are inevitable in relinquishment. Overall, such knowledge should enhance the child's feelings of self-worth and relieve the birth parent's guilt.

It is further argued that open adoption empowers the birth mother by offering her both choice and the feeling of being involved and in charge. In addition, a recognition of the altruism involved in giving up a baby may again help to lessen possible feelings of guilt. For example, in some African countries relatives who give a child to a sister or brother do not view it as a guilt-ridden gesture because their society does not view it in that light but, on the contrary, supports it – and the emotional impact of an experience largely depends on the cultural context within which it occurs. Open adoption may eventually bring about changes in social attitudes towards relinquishing mothers which do not convey shame, remorse or guilt.

A contrary argument put forward is that continued contact presents the mother with the opportunity for unending mourning, though Dominick[32] has found no evidence of this, at least in the relatively short follow-up period within which her study took place. It is similarly argued that, in meeting the adoptive parents, the birth parent may come to feel envy, rivalry and even anger towards the adopting couple because they can parent the child she is unable to care for. Such reactions are, after all, found among parents whose children go into foster care.

What relinquishing mothers may come to expect of open adoption is bound to vary. Whilst some will be content with simply meeting the adopters, others may be seeking periodic meetings or indeed life-long relationships. The matching of expectations can be crucial to the successful outcome of any arrangement. But matching itself will have to start with the child's best interests in mind, before considering those of the adults. Empirical evidence is lacking on most of the long-term effects of open adoption involving continued or periodic contact. The New Zealand study[33] does not suggest that many mothers seek lasting relationships with the adopting family, though this is more evident in anecdotal accounts of open adoption in the USA. It is to be hoped that the mother's involvement from the start in the selection of the adoptive parents, the possibility of continued contact, and the knowledge that her child is well looked after will help mitigate all the negative states found by different studies.

26

c) The adoptive parents

It is sometimes argued that the adoptive parents are the ones who have the least to gain from the practice of open adoption – that open adoption might even be a reason for turning to the apparent anonymity of inter-country adoptions. In the end, those who accept the idea of open adoption may not necessarily be the same type of person who previously went for traditional adoptions. The New Zealand experience again suggests that there is no shortage of couples prepared to take on adoption with continuing contact as far as infants are concerned.[34] The study adds, though, that birth mothers are happier with the idea of initial introductions than adoptive parents are, and that fewer adoptive parents welcome the idea of continued visits compared to birth mothers. It is still a matter of speculation whether adopters, by meeting the birth parent(s), feel thay have been given 'permission' to parent the child, leading to less anxious parenting. This assertion finds partial support from Dominick, who found that about a fifth of the adopters who met the birth mother said that the meeting 'positively affected their feelings about the child belonging in their family'.

Open adoption should, in theory, facilitate for the adopters the acknowledgement of difference and the reality of biological parenthood. It should also facilitate the resolution of possible feelings of loss connected with infertility, where this is present. Some would-be adopters will have experienced the loss of children through death, stillbirth or miscarriage: this may make it easier for them to understand the feelings, position and circumstances of parents who decide to give up a child, which in its turn should lead to more positive attitudes towards birth parents. It could equally be argued, of course, that continued contact might hinder the healing process.

Understandably, and irrespective of how well adoptive parents are prepared, they are also likely to carry many fears. These include fears about possible rejection, first by the agency and then by the mother. They may also experience stress arising from the knowledge that they are in competition with many others to adopt and, if they are successful, concern about their possible future relationship with the mother. Society provides no social script for such a relationship. A mother may take no fancy to a short, a fat, or a thin couple, or to a couple who happen to have an unusual name, or to one whose outlook on life appears different to her own. Caplan[35] asks whether

27

open adoption and its success depend on the optimistic notion that people can handle unfamiliar, even unprecedented, relationships.

Returning to an earlier point, concerning the degree to which a child can attach itself when faced with two possible sets of parents, the same question could now be reversed in relation to the adopting family: that is, can they successfully parent a child if they do not feel in full control? Some would argue that the concept of full control is a selfish form of parenting. On the other hand Kraft and colleagues[36] maintain that early contact with the birth parents constitutes interference or threat of interference for the adoptive parents. This could have a negative impact, such as undermining the adoptive parents' role and sense of security and eventually the quality of the relationship with the child. Our studies in Edinburgh suggest that being in charge and feeling legally secure is certainly necessary for whoever carries the parenting role. This security should be mostly provided from the knowledge that, legally, the child belongs in the adoptive family and that they should be in the position of regulating possible contacts. Children too, as we have found, need to feel the security provided by the adoption laws and they do not appear to feel, for example, that permanent foster care or indirectly, custodianship, provide full security.[37] It remains to be seen what the response of any of the parties will be to the new range of orders contained in the 1989 Children Act.

It is too early to say, too, what the impact of the new adoption law in the State of Victoria (Australia) is likely to be on adopters. This law provides not only for open adoption but also for continued contact where desired; furthermore, the consent of the birth parent(s) is required before the child is taken abroad. Other aspects of this legislation, and of that of Western Australia, make the adoption of older children almost impossible on the premise that it is undesirable to break the genetic link. Such a law, if introduced in Britain, would deprive over 2000 children a year of the security provided to them through adoption compared to that of long-term foster care, unless some other permanent legal status were to be introduced instead. As pointed out at the start of this chapter, the genetic link can still be maintained through adoption with contact. It is worth noting that the Torres Strait Islanders, while wishing to continue their tradition of open adoption, have also indicated to the relevant Australian Commission that they would welcome some legal security to protect

them from parental interference.[38] Reference was made earlier to the
expectations of each party and how some birth parent(s) may not be
content with the up-dating of information or with periodic meetings
but may be seeking a life-long, lasting relationship. Not all of those
who wish to adopt, as shown from Dominick's study,[39] are keen
for such a relationship, but others are. In such cases, the boundaries
between the two sets of families will have to be clearly negotiated
without the courts being dragged into what should essentially be
voluntary agreements.

When it comes to older children, we found in one of our recent
studies that the adopters were mostly unreceptive to the idea of
continuing contact.[40] These were people who had just adopted
children with special needs and had gone through many anxieties
before the making of the adoption order. Had we asked them
beforehand, they might have conveyed a different view. A few of them
qualified their response by adding that much would depend on what
kind of people the birth parents were. Whether the birth parents are
perceived as stable or potentially disruptive may indeed be decisive in
any arrangements. Links with siblings are generally far more
acceptable than links with parents. Not all older children requiring
new families need to maintain links, of course, but for those who do,
it is worth persevering to identify families who will accept inclusive
adoption. We have found that those with experience of fostering are
generally readier than others to do so.

The management of open adoption

The management of open adoption may present fewer problems and
concerns in Britain, where only approved agencies can arrange
adoptions, than in those countries, including some of the States of the
USA, where third-party adoptions are not only permissible but
apparently constitute the majority.

What we are seeing developing in some of the American States,
which must be avoided here, is a profit-motivated trade where the
interests of the children may or may not be served. In these areas, the
list of would-be adopters presented to the birth mother is first drawn
up by a private firm or agency employed by the couple and not by an
accredited body. The firm's interest is in packaging and 'selling' the
would-be adopters to the birth parent(s). Even in the controlled form
of semi-open adoption described by Fish and Speirs[41] in an accredited

agency, the study concluded that 'none of the participants had the child's interests as a clearly expressed priority. Many issues arise to distract the involved parties from what should be the overriding concern in placement decisions'. A private agency involved in open adoptions may be a firm of solicitors which attracts would-be adopters and birth parent(s) by placing advertisements in the press. These are meant to appeal to the expectant mother's feelings towards the unhappiness of childless couples.

When an expectant mother responds to an advert, a specially trained receptionist usually tries to make her feel welcome, refers to her altruism and praises her apparent generosity towards childless couples. From then on, psychological and other pressures, including financial inducements, are brought to bear. Stories emerging from some parts of the USA refer to birth mothers being met at airports in luxury limousines, booked into expensive hotels, having their college fees paid, and so on. Before the mother sees profiles of would-be adopters, the firm advises the couples on how to package themselves. The 'selling' of the prospective adopters starts with advice on how to present their portfolio, right down to the colour of paper they should use and the postures they should adopt in photographs. Depending on the information they have gathered from the mother, the agency advises the couple to stress, for example, their humour, their love of the theatre or animals, or their interest in outdoor sports. Several profile drafts may be prepared before the final one is selected. The preparation process ends with an instruction to the would-be adopters to role-play their introduction to the birth parent(s).

It is not unusual to read of a mother who selected a couple because of their profession, or the type of dog or house they had. Caplan[42] describes how a couple with a black poodle that was shown in the photographs wearing red sunglasses were picked by a birth mother who loved dogs, rather than for their anticipated parenting qualities. After the paper selection follow face-to-face meetings before the arrangement is finalised. Depending on circumstances and preferences, the expectant mother may move hundreds of miles to take up residence near or even with the prospective adopters until confinement. She may ask for the adopters to be present at the confinement and to take the child home afterwards. The type of contact that develops from then on depends on negotiations already carried out, though views can change. Whilst some birth parent(s) only wish to have a single contact or simply to keep in touch by letter or phone, others seek closer relationships. Accounts given in newsletters refer to birth parent(s) baby-sitting for the adopting couple or going on holiday together. It is not certain whether this suggests difficulties on the part of the birth parent(s) in separating from the child, which could undermine the adopters, or whether it is to be expected of a relationship developing between two families being brought together through adoption.

Anecdotal accounts from the States refer to mothers changing their minds, thus causing considerable distress to would-be adopters, especially after such an intensive relationship. Statistical information, however, is in short supply. Prospective adopters usually invest considerable emotion in getting to know the mother, sometimes offering her accommodation and even holding her hand during the birth. We also know from studies that would-be adopters feel it as a loss even when an agency has simply described a possible child to them, when later they are told that the mother has changed her mind. In the case of open adoption, the investment is much bigger and, equally, the distress following a change of mind more devastating. For the mother, too, the decision is likely to increase her sense of guilt and betrayal towards people she came to know in person and to whom she feels responsible.

Obviously, not all States in the USA are adult-centred in their adoption policies and practices. And we must ensure that aspects of the profit-packaging approach described above do not creep into adoption practice in Britain under the guise of openness, and that we manage open adoption here in a way that continues to have the child's interests as paramount. To pretend, though, that because third-party adoptions are prohibited, some of the American excesses cannot happen here, is to fly in the face of evidence. For example, an increasing number of people are successful in bringing children from other countries into the UK for adoption without the involvement of an approved agency. One such couple, in a recent letter to *The Scotsman* (22/09/90) implied that, though they may be creating problems for the child, it is up to the professionals to provide the necessary counselling and other services to deal with these!

Arranging open or semi-open adoptions is likely to present accredited agencies with initial problems until they develop practice experience. However, agencies could start planning now for the kind

31

of programmes that will be necessary in the handling of open adoption and adoption with contact for older children. Such programmes, for would-be adopters and birth parents, would have to consider such issues as: offering counselling to both parties to establish their wishes; preparing agreed profiles; establishing and matching preferences; supporting couples who inevitably will only make it as far as the short-list; identifying the best point for introductions which neither compromises the mother's decision nor exposes would-be adopters to unnecessary pain; managing the possible presence of the adopters at the child's birth; picking up the pieces when either party changes their mind; becoming involved in continued up-dating of records with information obtained from both parties (which should have already been happening); and, in the case of continued contact, being prepared to act as mediator when access arrangements have broken down.

Final thoughts

Though there is still a great deal to be learnt, open adoption is inevitable in a society that is increasingly becoming more open and sensitive to the needs of all the parties involved in adoption. Though some problems previously faced by adopted people and birth parents in a closed system of adoption are expected to decrease through open placements, we do not know whether unanticipated issues will emerge. On balance, the available evidence is in favour of greater openness in adoption and of the need for older children to maintain meaningful links with birth relatives.' As far as baby adoptions are concerned, there seems to be agreement about the desirability for mothers to have much more say in the selection of would-be adopters, provided it is from a short-list screened by an accredited agency. There is, equally, considerable agreement about the desirability for introductory meetings, but there is more uncertainty about the management impact, and about the implications and outcome of continued contact. Judgement on these has to be reserved until more practice experience and empirical evidence are accumulated. Different types of contact will eventually have to be evaluated in relation to their meaning for each of the three parties involved. McRoy[43] concludes from her studies that the greatest benefit and the least risk seem to occur in families with semi-open adoption.

To maintain the integrity of adoption as an institution, agencies will have to develop preparatory programmes for the two parties on how to handle openness. Agencies should also retain the right to draw up short-lists of would-be adopters with the interests of the child as the paramount consideration, from which list the mother can make her choice. This process, whilst empowering mothers, also gives more power to agencies than ever before, which they will have to exercise responsibly. The history of adoption is tainted with class bias. Open adoption, like inter-country adoption, has the potential of pushing adoption further in this direction. For example, in many of the American States, open adoption and inter-country adoption operate almost exclusively in favour of those who are demonstrably well off and 'nice people'. The danger of two-tier adoption is as real here as in the States. Already, a pattern is beginning to develop here with the better-off adopting in-country and inter-country healthy infants, whilst the rest are urged to adopt children with special needs, possibly with an allowance attached. We will need to decide whether this is the system we want for the future.

References

1 Department of Health 'Inter-departmental review of adoption law: discussion paper no. 1: The nature and effect of adoption' HMSO, 1990.

2 McWhinnie A *Adopted children: how they grow up* Routledge & Kegan Paul, 1967.

3 Triseliotis J *In search of origins* Routledge & Kegan Paul, 1973.

4 Craig M 'Adoption – not a big deal' Department of Social Policy and Social Work, Edinburgh University, 1990.

5 Pannor R and Barran A 'Open adoption as standard practice' *Child Welfare* LXIII 3, 1984.

6 Winkler R and van Keppel M 'Relinquishing mothers in adoption' Melbourne: Institute of Family Studies, 1984.

7 Bouchier P, Lambert L and Triseliotis J *Parting with a child for adoption* BAAF, 1991.

8 Millen L and Roll S 'Solomon's mothers: a special case of pathological bereavement' *Amer J Orthopsychiat* 53 3, 1985.

9 Parkes C M *Bereavement* Tavistock Publications, 1972.

10 Deykin E, Campbell P and Sorosky A 'Birth parents who relinquished babies for adoption revisited' *Family process* 17 3, 1984.

33

11 Triseliotis J 'Adoption with contact' *Adoption & Fostering* 9 4, 1985.
Triseliotis J 'Maintaining the links in adoption' *British Journal of Social Work*, 1991.

12 Fratter J 'Family placement and access' Barnardo's, 1989.

13 Kirk H D *Shared fate*, New York: Free Press of Glencoe, 1964.

14 Fish A and Speirs C 'Biological parents choose adoptive parents: the use of profiles in adoption' *Child welfare* LXIX 2, 1990.

15 Triseliotis J and Russell J *Hard to place* Gower, 1984.
See also 3 above.

16 Dominick C 'Early contact in adoption: contact between birth mothers and adoptive parents at the time of and after the adoption' Research Series no 10, Wellington: Department of Social Welfare, 1988.

17 Goldstein J, Freud A and Solnit A J *Beyond the best interests of the child* New York: Free Press, 1973.
Goldstein J, Freud A and Solnit A J *Before the best interests of the child* Burnett Books/Andre Deutsch, 1980.

18 Keshet H F and Rosenthal K M *Fathers without partners* New Jersey: Rowan and Littlefield, 1980.

19 Furstenberg F F 'The new extended family: the experience of parents and children after marriage' in Pasley E and Ihinger-Tallman M (eds) *Remarriage and step-parenting* New York: Guildford, 1987.

20 Schaffer H R *Making decisions about children* Basil Blackwell, 1990.

21 Borland M, O'Hara G and Triseliotis J 'Permanency planning for children in Lothian Region' Report to Social Work Services Group and Lothian Region, 1989.
Wedge P and Mantle G 'Sibling groups in social work' Department of Social Work, University of East Anglia, 1990.
See also 12 above.

22 Beckett J 'Adoption in three Torres Strait communities' unpublished manuscript quoted by Ban ZP 'The application of the Queensland Adoption Act 1964-1988 to the traditional adoption practice of Torres Strait Islanders' MSW thesis, University of Melbourne, 1989.

23 Fox N 'Attachment of Kibbutz infants to mother and metapelet' *Child development* 48, 1977.

24 Schaffer H R *Mothering* Fontana Open Books, 1977.

25 See 12 and 21 above.

26 Hill M, Lambert L and Triseliotis J *Achieving adoption with love and money* National Children's Bureau, 1989.

27 See 11 above.

28 See 5, 6 and 7 above.

29 See 6 above.

30 See 7 above.

31 See 5 above.

32 See 16 above.

33 See 16 above.

34 See 16 above.

35 Caplan A 'A reporter at large' *The New Yorker* 21 May and 28 May, 1990.

36 Kraft A D, Palombo J, Woods P K, Mitchell O and Schmit A W 'Some theoretical considerations on confidential adoptions. Part I: the birth mother' *Child and adolescent social work* 2 1, 1985.
    Kraft A D, Palombo J, Woods P K, Mitchell O and Schmit A W 'The birth mother' *Child and adolescent social work* 2 2, 1985.
    Kraft A D, Palombo J, Woods P K, Mitchell O and Schmit A W 'The birth mother' *Child and adolescent social work* 2 3, 1985.

37 Triseliotis J 'Identity and security in adoption and long-term fostering' *Adoption & Fostering* 7 1, 1983.
    Triseliotis J and Hill M 'Children and adoption allowances' *Adoption and Fostering* 11 1, 1987.

38 Ban Z P 'The application of the Queensland Adoption Act 1964-1988 to the traditional adoption practice of Torres Strait islanders' MSW thesis, University of Melbourne, 1989.

39 See 16 above.

40 Lambert L, Buist M, Triseliotis J and Hill M *Freeing children for adoption* BAAF, 1990.

41 See 14 above.

42 See 35 above.

43 McRoy R 'Openness in adoption' Monograph, School of Social Work, University of Texas, 1988. Referred to by Caplan (see 35).

2 Adoptive parents and open adoption in the UK

Joan Fratter

The material on which this chapter is based derives from interviews undertaken in 1987 with adoptive parents in 22 families who had experience of open placements. Their perspective was sought as part of a Cranfield Institute research study concerned with the achievement of permanency for children in touch with birth parents.[1] All the adoptive parents lived in England, the majority (in 19 families) in the south of England and East Anglia. Two adoptive families were living in the north west and one in the north of England.

Background to the research

Source of the sample
The study was built on the 1986 survey by Thoburn and Rowe of 1,165 placements of children with special needs made by 24 voluntary agencies between January 1980 and December 1984.[2] Thoburn and Rowe found that, although 20 per cent of the children were said to have needed to maintain contact with birth parents at the time of placement, this had been achieved for only ten per cent. It emerged that six of the 24 agencies had placed no children who had had continued contact (defined as actual meetings) or links (defined as other forms of communication) with birth parents or other relatives after placement. Only 33 of the 117 children who were said to be having continued contact with birth parents were described as having been adopted. Sixty-one were permanently fostered and 23 were being fostered with a view to adoption.

The placing agencies
Interviews were also undertaken in 1987 by the author with representatives of 22 of the 24 voluntary adoption agencies, one in Scotland, one in Wales and the remainder in England. The aim was to gain some impression of how they were attempting to achieve both permanence and continuing links with birth relatives. There were

wide variations between agencies in relation to the extent to which they had explored alternatives to the closed adoption model.

On the basis of the interviews with agency workers, a comparison was made between the ten agencies which had placed children who had maintained contact with birth parents after adoption and the 12 agencies which had not done so. There were significant differences between the attitudes and practices of these two groups of agencies.

Howell and Ryburn[3] have emphasised that a key aspect of the closed model of adoption is the powerful role of the social worker or agency and the limited participation of birth and adoptive parents. It was clear from the responses of agency representatives that some of those with no, or very limited, experience of openness were anxious about handing over too much 'responsibility', particularly to birth parents but also, to a more limited extent, to adoptive parents. They felt it was important to 'protect' adoptive and birth parents from extra pressures at an emotionally difficult time, unless they themselves had requested this and were thought to be capable of handling the situation. On the other hand, for some agencies, it was the exception for adoptive and birth parents *not* to meet. It was only in rare circumstances that, after counselling, birth parents chose not to take up the opportunity to meet adoptive parents. The latter, however, were prepared from the outset of their relationship with the agency to anticipate the possibility of a meeting. Clearly, the preparation and counselling given to adoptive and birth parents were significant, as was the degree of confidence the agency had in setting up such arrangements.

Some agencies anticipated an increase in the number of more open adoptions where parents were voluntarily relinquishing the care of a child with disabilities – there seemed to be something of the notion of the 'deserving' as against the 'undeserving' parent, as well as the child having less potential for manipulation in the future.

The sample of adoptive parents
This chapter is chiefly concerned with that aspect of the study which encompassed interviews with adoptive parents. These were conducted with 22 families whose adopted children had maintained some form of contact or link with birth parents since the placement for adoption. The aim was to gain some understanding of their perspective as participants in an adoption arrangement which, in 1987, was

relatively unusual in the UK. Arrangements in which children and young people have maintained some contact with relatives other than birth parents are more common. The study focused on placements with birth parental contact, however, because the potential for role conflict and the reluctance of agencies to consider continuing contact are much greater in those situations.

It was initially anticipated that the sample would be drawn from the 23 adoptive families identified in the Thoburn and Rowe survey[4] as having continued contact with birth parents after adoption. These 23 families between them had adopted 33 children placed by ten of the voluntary adoption agencies. The agency representatives were contacted in September 1987 and asked to consider approaching the adoptive parents of the children identified in the survey on behalf of the researcher. In the event, either because the family did not respond to the approach by the agency (four families) or because the agency did not consider it appropriate to approach the family (eight families), only 11 of those families whose children had been identified through the survey were included in the sample. Of the four families who did not respond to the approach from the agency, representatives were not aware in three instances of the adoptive parents experiencing any difficulties in relation to contact. However, in the fourth case, there had been lengthy and difficult legal proceedings in which the issue of access had been significant. There was a range of reasons why agency representatives did not think it appropriate to approach adoptive parents in eight families but these matters were not related to contact. Therefore, in only one instance as far as the researcher was made aware, were there features in relation to the families not included in the study which distinguished them from those who were.

In addition to the 11 families identified through the Thoburn and Rowe survey, a further 11 families were recruited to the study. Adoptive parents in five families had had children placed with them by the participating agencies but the placements had not been included in the earlier survey. Adoptive parents in a further four families were contacted via the network of Parent-to-Parent Information on Adoption Services. A further two families were interviewed following an approach to the researcher by a local authority social worker who knew of the study and believed that they could appropriately be included. The adoptive parents in the 22 families were generous in giving their time and sharing their experiences. Adoptive parents in 18 families were interviewed in their own home and, in one case, in the office of the placing agency. Three adoptive parents were interviewed by telephone because the distance made a personal visit impracticable. In 15 of the interviews, both adoptive parents participated. The three telephone interviews took place with the adoptive mothers only. Two of the adoptive parents interviewed in person were single women. In two instances the adoptive father was not available to be present during an interview at home, in both cases because of work commitments. During the course of the interviews in the homes of adoptive parents, the researcher met 15 of the adopted children included in the study. Only six, however, took part to any extent in the discussions (it had been the choice of the adoptive parents to include them).

The children

There were 32 children in the sample study, of whom 30, according to the description given by the agency social worker and/or the adoptive parents, had special needs as defined by Thoburn and Rowe for their survey. These included a physical disability and/or learning difficulties, and/or factors arising from a difficult family background or from the effects of adverse experiences while in care. The two children who were described as not having any of these special needs were a girl and a boy relinquished voluntarily by their birth mother as infants and placed directly with their adoptive parents.

The 'problem' factors affecting children adopted from care included a history of multiple moves or changes of care-giver, at least one previous disrupted placement, 'institutionalisation', a history of deprivation or abuse, behaviour difficulties, and emotional problems. Fifteen of the children were affected by four or five of these factors. One child who did not present any emotional or behaviour difficulties at placement was needing to be placed with an older sibling who had experienced multiple moves. Their parents suffered from mental illness and had problems relating to drug abuse.

The characteristics of the 32 children and features of their care histories are summarised below:

Age at time of interview with adoptive parents (1987)

Range: 2½ years up to 20 years:

Aged under 8 years	7
Aged 9 to 15 years	18
Aged 16+	7

Gender

Boys	19
Girls	13

Ethnic background

White	22
Black (mainly Afro-Caribbean)	10

Siblings

Single children	16
Siblings (2) placed together	14
Siblings (2) placed separately	2

Route to placement for adoption

Voluntarily relinquished by single birth mothers	2
Adoption requested by birth parents because of severe disability or learning difficulties (children aged from birth to 10 years at placement)	6
Plan for adoption made after admission to care	24
'Compulsorily' in care	22
In voluntary care	2

Expectations concerning parental agreement to adoption at the time of placement

Birth parents had requested adoption	8
Agreement anticipated	6
Agreement not anticipated:	
expected to contest	16
expected to withhold agreement	2

Age at last separation from one or both birth parents

Aged 3 years or under (including eight under 12 months)	17
Aged 4 to 10 years	14
Aged 10+	1

Length of time in care at placement

Up to 12 months	13
Five years plus (including one child who spent 13 years in the same children's home)	5

Age at placement

Aged 5 years or under	12
11 to 14 years	5

It is important to note that 22 of the children were compulsorily in care prior to adoption and that parental agreement was not anticipated at the time of placement in relation to adoption for 18 children. Thus these were placements with potential for conflict. Packman *et al*[5] and Millham *et al*[6] have described the significance of the route to care in affecting the likelihood of the agency being able to work co-operatively with birth parents.

A further surprising feature of the children in the study was that more than half (17) had been last separated from their birth parents when aged three years or under – they were not predominantly the older group of children described by Triseliotis[7] and Thoburn.[8] Indeed, at placement, only five children were aged 11 or older.

Characteristics of the adopters

Among the adoptive parents there were 20 married couples and two single women (one widowed after the placement for adoption and one divorced before placement). One couple described themselves as having a 'mixed-race marriage' in that one partner was 'Black West Indian' and the other white. They had adopted a boy of Afro-Caribbean parentage. Nine of the children had been placed trans-racially, reflecting the fact that most of the placements had been made prior to 1984, before agencies generally had begun to pursue a policy of seeking adoptive parents of the same ethnic background as the child.

The composition of the families is summarised below:

- adoptive parents in 14 families had had no children born to them

- adoptive parents in 14 families had other adopted children, or foster children, or children born to them, in addition to the children included in the study

- adoptive parents in nine families had had experience of both open and closed adoption

- adoptive parents in three families had adopted unrelated children in the study and so were in touch with two sets of birth parents.

Degree of openness

The nature and extent of contact at the time of interview varied widely. This variation derived in part from the fact that 'contact' had been defined by social workers or adoptive parents themselves and also because, with the passage of time, there had been changes; at the time of the interviews the children had been in placement for periods ranging from six months to 13 years.

The experience of adoptive parents ranged from one or two meetings with birth parent(s) with, subsequently, links or the possibility of links, through to placements in which birth parents were welcome and regular visitors to the home of the adoptive family.

Most adoptive families had a level of contact between these two extremes. Only two adoptive families were having no contact of any sort with birth parents (although one adoptive couple was willing to exchange information and the other couple had recently requested, on behalf of their two children, a meeting with their birth mother).

Adoptive parents in six families, caring for seven children, were maintaining links by means of letters, telephone calls, gifts, photographs and cards. Adoptive parents in four of these six families had met birth relatives at least once since adoption and did not exclude the possibility of future meetings. Parents in 14 families had adopted 21 children who were having face-to-face contact with one or both birth parents. The frequency of such contact ranged from once every three to four weeks to once or twice a year. All the adoptive parents in the study had met one or both parents of their adopted children at least once, in most cases either before or during the introductions. In all cases where contact was occurring, this was by mutual agreement. There were no instances in the study of adoption orders with a condition of contact attached.

In looking at the extent of contact, it is important to emphasise that it was the attitude of the adoptive parents, rather than the degree of contact, which determined how 'open' the placement felt. The openness of attitude of the adoptive parents was assessed using eight attributes which are important in all adoption placements but particularly so in adoption with contact:

- being able to appreciate adoption from the child's perspective

- acknowledging the importance of the birth family to the child's sense of identity

- feeling comfortable in discussing adoption

- acknowledging the difference between adoptive parenting and biological parenting

- being able to express some understanding of the feelings of birth parents

- having a non-judgmental attitude towards the birth family

- seeking positive traits in birth parents

– having a positive view about contact between the child and birth parents, where this seemed appropriate for the child.

Using these criteria, adoptive parents in 20 of the 22 families were seen as particularly open in attitude. They shared in varying degrees the generosity of spirit and the inclusiveness of the adoptive mother who said: 'When you love your children this must extend to the parents as well'. However, adoptive parents in two families expressed some resentment about being involved in an open placement, even though both had known from the outset that this was the plan. They indicated some unease about their children's contact with their birth parents which, they acknowledged, was not solely related to its impact on the children. Adoptive parents in one family had not met the birth mother of their adopted son, even though he had requested this. They had met his birth father but contact had not continued. The boy was taken by a social worker to meet his birth mother on neutral territory. Although this might be termed an 'open adoption' because contact with the birth mother had continued, the situation did not feel at all open on the basis of the discussion with the adoptive parents. By contrast, there were two children, aged 10 and 12, placed five years earlier, who had had no direct links or contact since soon after placement. However, the adoptive parents were very open in their attitude: they included the girls in the interview and encouraged them to get out their life-story books and show photographs and letters written by their birth mother. The girls seemed completely at ease in talking about the circumstances of their adoption and about their birth mother.

Who initiated openness

The researcher sought information as to how the adoptive parents had become involved in an adoption placement with a degree of openness – a particularly relevant issue in view of the frequent assumption that such adoptive parents cannot be recruited. It emerged that preparation by the agency had had considerable impact on prospective adoptive parents, both in terms of openness of attitude and with regard to the possibility of their maintaining some form of contact after adoption. Most of the adoptive parents said that working with the agency had helped them to understand the importance of the family of origin to the child. In only four families had the adoptive parents approached an agency with some expectation of openness. Adoptive parents in 14 families felt they had definitely been influenced by the agency in forming a more open attitude.

In view of the fact that most adoptive parents had approached agencies with an expectation of a traditional, closed model of adoption, it is interesting that adoptive parents in 13 families had either offered to maintain contact or had initiated contact, although this had not been part of the agency's plan at the time of placement. For example, the birth parents of a girl with learning difficulties who had been placed in an adoptive family at the age of nine with no provision for continuing links, had enquired about her progress from the placing agency about six months after the adoption order had been granted. On learning of their enquiry, the adoptive mother had invited the birth parents and their other three children to visit. Thereafter, a pattern of contact had been maintained whereby members of the birth family, including on one occasion a grandmother, had visited twice a year.

Adopters' experiences of openness

Adoptive parents were asked to describe their overall feelings about having been involved in an adoption with some degree of contact. Adoptive parents in 16 families (with 24 adopted children in the study) felt positive or very positive, and were able to perceive benefits for themselves and their children. In half of these families, contact had been or was being maintained through links, directly or via the agency, but without contact.

In the remaining eight families who felt positively, there was ongoing face-to-face contact with one or both parents and, in six families, with other birth relatives as well. All these adoptive parents were especially open in attitude and regarded adoption in terms of a 'gift' rather than a 'rescue'. All were able to acknowledge that adoption entailed an experience of loss for the child and the birth parents. This attitude was demonstrated by comments such as:

> Shelley has enabled us to have children. She's generous. The children [aged seven and six] thanked her for having agreed to their adoption.

The adoptive parents in eight of those 16 families had adopted one or more children in addition to those included in the study, who did not have continuing contact with birth parents (although some had links with other members of the family of origin). In four families, the adoptive parents had experienced a traditional closed adoption in that they had not at any stage met birth relatives and there were no other links. Children in those four families had been placed as babies, having been voluntarily relinquished by their birth mothers. Adoptive parents in the other four families had either been able to maintain links with other relatives or had met the birth parent(s) of their children on one occasion. There was a strong preference for a more open model of adoption among those eight adoptive families.

Reservations were expressed by adoptive parents in six families. In two families there had been difficulties in the past, in three families some tensions or problems were currently being experienced, and in one family there were no specific concerns about contact but, rather, a general sense of unease. These six families had adopted eight children, all but one of whom were having infrequent face-to-face contact. The exception was a teenage girl who, at her own request, no longer had face-to-face contact but whose brother, placed in the same adoptive home, had continued to meet their birth mother. Two of these six families were assessed by the researcher as 'less open' in attitude. One adoptive mother was very clear about the social and material advantages of adoption and described the extensive range of hobbies, interests and foreign holidays her adopted children were able to enjoy.

She commented: 'She [the birth mother] ought to appreciate the fact that we have been able to give them chances they would never have had if they had not been adopted'. The other 'less open' adoptive parents conveyed a sense of unease about the contact between their adopted son, placed at 13 years of age and his birth mother. This family had, many years earlier, adopted three children as babies on the closed model. They implied a preference for this arrangement, even though they did not believe that contact had adversely affected their relationship with their son.

Adopters' attachment to the child
Two key aspects of the emotional development of adoptive parents are their capacity to become attached to the child and their sense of entitlement.

In terms of attachment, none of the adoptive parents, including those who had had some reservations about maintaining links, thought that their attachment to the child had been delayed or impaired because of the contact. There were some, indeed, who thought that contact with birth parents had brought them closer to their child, particularly in the earlier stages of the placement, because this had increased their understanding about the circumstances leading to adoption. A couple who had adopted two unrelated boys, each of whom had continuing contact with his birth mother, contrasted the two situations. With the placement of their first child, they had not met the birth mother until several months after placement. With hindsight, they felt this had been a disadvantage because his birth mother was so important to Richard. Subsequently, before Robert was placed with them, they had been able to arrange to meet his birth mother during the introductions. They felt this had been a considerable advantage in enabling them to develop an attachment.

Factors associated with a sense of entitlement

'Entitlement' encompasses the feeling by adoptive parents that adoption was right for the child and for the birth parents as well as for themselves. There were several ways in which adoptive parents in the study felt that their sense of entitlement had been enhanced through contact.

Contact breaking down opposition to adoption

Adoptive parents in 16 families had met the birth parents who were giving their approval to placement. This included adoptive parents in six families who believed that, without continuing links, the opposition the birth parents had expressed towards adoption at the outset of the placement would have been likely to have continued. An example is the situation of Michael and Sarah, who had been placed with their adoptive parents in particularly contentious circumstances. Both children had been removed at birth on Place of Safety Orders from the care of their parents because of a history of mental illness and drug abuse. Eventually, when the children were aged seven weeks and 15 months respectively, they were placed with prospective adoptive parents. During protracted legal proceedings, the children met their birth parents while being escorted by a social worker to a social work office. Eventually, because of the distress this caused the children, the adoptive parents, against the advice of the family social worker, invited the birth parents to visit the adoptive home. Over time, a good relationship was established and the birth mother indicated that she would give her agreement to the adoption, but only if interviewed by the reporting officer in the home of the adoptive parents. She mistrusted authority and wanted to make it absolutely clear that she was only giving her agreement to adoption by the children's present carers. The birth father was not required to give agreement because the children were born outside marriage.

Adopters chosen by birth parents

In five families, the adoptive parents had either been chosen by the birth parents or agreement had been given to adoption only because of the birth parents' confidence in them. Leon's birth mother, for example, had tried to care for him as a single parent but, after some months, she approached an adoption agency, believing that this would be best for his long-term welfare. Because the placement was to be a direct one from the birth mother, and because the bond she had with her son made it important that the birth mother felt happy about the adoption arrangements, the agency agreed to involve her in the choice of adoptive parents. The birth mother felt uneasy after meeting the first couple selected by the agency and was therefore introduced to a second couple. The adoptive mother described how she and her husband and the birth mother immediately felt a sense of warmth and rapport. The decision was made for the birth mother when Leon crawled over to the adoptive mother in a confident way. The adoptive parents, who had not been able to receive in this way the approval of the birth parents of the other children they had adopted, commented: 'We felt good to know that Hyacinth had specifically chosen us'.

Improved circumstances of birth parents

Some adoptive parents cited the fact that through continuing contact they were aware that birth parents' circumstances had improved. This is relevant to a sense of entitlement in that adoptive parents can be adversely affected if they feel they have been party to depriving a birth parent of his or her child wrongfully, or that a birth parent may be experiencing continued distress because of the loss of the child. This may be illustrated by a couple who had adopted a baby boy with Down's Syndrome. They had been very aware of the sadness of the birth mother when they met the birth parents prior to placement. The adoptive mother had felt that the birth mother would not have wanted to part with her son for adoption had her husband been more supportive. Two years later, via the social services department, the adoptive parents initiated a meeting with the birth parents, feeling that it would be helpful to the birth mother to be reassured about the little boy's progress. By the time of the meeting, the birth parents had given birth to another son and the birth mother seemed much happier in herself, as well as having indeed been reassured by the meeting. The adoptive mother explained to the researcher that she did not appreciate until after that meeting how 'haunted' she herself had been by the sadness of the birth mother. The meeting had therefore been enormously helpful to her, in that she no longer had to picture the birth mother as a sad and unhappy woman.

Benefits of contact in legally complex cases
Adoptive parents in four families had encountered difficulties in that the birth parents had agreed at a very late stage to the adoption application after protracted legal proceedings. There was a feeling that their agreement had been less than wholehearted. The adoptive parents felt, however, that continuing contact had prevented a contested adoption. Contact had also enabled the adoptive parents to form a judgement about the importance of adoption for the child. In two other cases, birth parents had not been in agreement with adoption: in one case, a freeing application made by the local authority had been opposed and in another, agreement to the adoption application had been withheld although not actively opposed. As a result of contact, both sets of adoptive parents felt they understood the reasons for the birth parents being unable to give agreement. Thus, to some extent, they felt that contact mitigated the difficulties associated with adoptions without parental agreement.

Alleged drawbacks of contact for adopters
In addition to the threat to entitlement, it has been suggested that contact after adoption can be distressing to adoptive parents by reinforcing the knowledge that the child was not born to them, by instilling a fear of the birth parents abusing their knowledge of the child's whereabouts, and by engendering feelings of rivalry and resentment about sharing the child.

A reminder of childlessness

Adoptive parents in 14 families had not had a child born to them. There are opposing views as to whether, on the one hand, an adoption with contact is helpful in preventing adoptive parents from denying the difference between adoptive and biological parenthood or whether, on the other, it detracts from their ability to develop an attachment to the child by keeping open the wound of infertility. This was not, however, seen as a difficult issue by adoptive parents in 11 of the families. But two adoptive parents directly, and one indirectly, acknowledged that continuing contact was, or had been, a painful reminder of childlessness.

One adoptive father acknowledged having found this more difficult than his wife in the early stages of placement. It had emphasised his sense of 'guilt' at not being able to give his wife a child. However, he had overcome this with the help and understanding of his wife and because of his confidence in the security of the relationship they had with their adopted child. Another adoptive father admitted that, when the birth parents first had contact in the adoptive home, he had avoided being there when they visited because he did not want to acknowledge that the children had parents who had given them birth. He had gradually become reconciled to this, however, as he did not experience the birth parents' visits as any threat in reality. An adoptive mother indirectly acknowledged that contact with her daughters' birth mother raised the issue of infertility for her, when she explained that her husband did not feel jealous or resentful of the birth parents because he had had children born to him in a previous marriage whereas she had not.

Thus, on the basis of the information offered to the researcher by adoptive parents, it seemed that only one adoptive parent found continuing contact still an issue in respect of her not having given birth to her adopted children herself.

Turning up on the doorstep

The fear of birth parents abusing knowledge of the whereabouts of the adoptive child was a reason given by the Houghton Committee[9] for maintaining confidentiality in adoption placements. Birth parents had identifying information in respect of 16 adoptive families in the present study.

Parents in ten adoptive families, caring for 15 children, had invited the birth parents to visit their home at least once and 11 birth families had visited on several occasions. None expressed anxiety about birth families visiting too frequently or turning up unexpectedly. However, one couple had felt concerned, unnecessarily they now realised, in the early stages of the placement when the birth family had moved nearer their home, and another mother said she was quite relieved that the birth mother was now being cared for in a residential setting at some distance away, because of her mental deterioration. Birth parents were aware of the name and telephone number, and probably the address, of six adoptive families. One adoptive family had received what they regarded as inappropriate phone calls in the early stages of the placement.

Adoptive parents in six families did not believe that the birth parents had identifying information about them so the question of their feeling anxious about possible 'interference' by birth parents did not arise. However, one adoptive father commented that, had the birth parent 'turned up on the doorstep' early on in the placement five years before this would have been problematic, but they now felt confident they could handle that unlikely possibility.

Overall, the adoptive parents whose identity was known seemed not to feel threatened by the lack of anonymity – possibly because most of them had chosen to allow birth parents to have identifying information. Many enjoyed 'a relationship of trust and confidence' because sufficient time had elapsed for them to feel confident that abuse of their trust was unlikely.

Potential for rivalry

The possibility of feelings of rivalry between adoptive and birth parents is often cited as a reason to avoid contact with birth parents after adoption, but not with other birth relatives with whom the same feelings of rivalry may not exist.

Adoptive parents in six families, none of whom had had children born to them, acknowledged having experienced some rivalry in the past, usually with the birth parent of the same sex. However, for only one couple was there still some element of this in the relationship with the birth family.

The adoptive mother of Gary, placed at the age of nine, explained that she had experienced some rivalry with the birth mother as her relationship with Gary deepened. This had been exacerbated by Gary repeating alleged remarks made by his birth mother which were critical of his adoptive mother – for example, her being too strict. The adoptive mother described how she had often felt quite hurt. There had never been any rivalry between the birth mother and the adoptive father. The adoptive parents felt there had been less tension between the birth mother and the adoptive mother over time and they adopted a generous attitude towards the birth mother, believing the problems she had created by encouraging Gary to see the two mothers as rivals resulted from her not understanding Gary's needs rather than from malicious motives. The adoptive parents went to considerable efforts to ensure that Gary had face-to-face contact with his mother twice a year.

Adoptive parents in five families described feelings of rivalry which had been dissipated by the initial or subsequent meetings with birth parents.

Whether contact entailed sharing information through letters and photographs or participating in face-to-face meetings, adoptive parents were to a greater or lesser degree sharing the child and according a special place to the birth parents. Adoptive parents were asked whether they found this difficult, in particular whether it had become harder as the child became more integrated emotionally into the family as time passed. An adoptive parent in only one family acknowledged that it had become harder for her to feel positively about contact with her sons' birth mother and that in fact her resentment about their still seeing her had increased. No other families described this as a problem for them at the time of the interviews.

Some adoptive parents said they had never found sharing the child to be difficult while others stated that sharing the child had become easier with the passing of time, as they themselves had begun to feel more secure as adoptive parents and they had evidence of the child's attachment to them.

Socio-economic status and race

Most of the adoptive parents had little in common with their adopted child's birth parent(s) in terms of education, occupation and income (but it was not the case in every instance, as is usually supposed, that the adoptive parents enjoyed the more favoured socio-economic status). In general, this did not appear to have created any major tensions. Adoptive parents in six of the 22 families had adopted transracially, and for some this increased the value they placed on contact with birth parents. Transracial adopters in five families were among the group who felt positively about open adoption. The sixth couple were 'less open' adopters who felt generally uneasy, though they did not identify race as an aspect of this. Their son, who was of mixed parentage, was maintaining contact with his white birth mother.

Adopters' views of the impact of contact on their children

It appeared to the researcher that it had been their child-centred focus which had enabled the parents in the 22 adoptive families to become involved in an adoption with contact. Their perception of the impact of contact on their adopted children was therefore an important determinant of their overall attitude to the experience of open adoption.

In all but one of the 22 families, the adoptive parents felt that their children had gained some benefit from contact or links with birth parents. This included four couples who had described some problems associated with contact. Areas discussed with the adoptive parents were the child's sense of identity, understanding of the circumstances of adoption and his/her feeling free to attach to the adoptive parents. The adopted person not thought by his adopted parents to have benefited from contact was an older teenager, placed at the age of ten after many years in residential care. His ambivalent feelings and confusion were compounded by his awareness of his birth mother's disapproval, although she had actually given her agreement to the adoption. At an earlier stage in the placement, contact had been terminated but subsequently reinstated. (He had been placed with an older sister who was thought to have gained from contact.)

Adopters' views on the impact of contact on birth parents

The experience of adoption with contact for adoptive parents was closely related to the attitude of the birth parents to the adoption, the role they fulfilled, and the relationships established within the adoption triangle. For this reason, the researcher sought the observations of adoptive families as to how they thought birth parents had been affected by the opportunity of maintaining contact. Although this information is indirect, in an area where first-hand views are still rarely recorded it may be thought to be of value.

Adoptive parents in 13 families (including adoptive parents in three families who were each in touch with two sets of birth parents, having adopted unrelated children) felt able to comment on the impact on birth parents. Only two of the adoptive parents in this group described some difficulties in the past in relation to contact or the attitude of birth parents. By the time of the interview, however, these difficulties had been overcome. All the adoptive parents in this group expressed warm feelings towards the birth parents. They believed that all the birth parents had benefited in terms of accepting their loss. In the view of the adoptive parents, the birth parents' process of grieving and adjustment had been helped by their having direct knowledge of the adoptive family, by being able to picture the child, and by knowing that the child wished to be adopted. A number of adoptive parents mentioned that the benefit of open adoption had not only been that the birth parents had withdrawn their opposition, but also that they appeared to have been more comfortable about the adoption.

Adoptive parents who did not feel able to comment on the feelings of birth parents were those who had either had very limited contact with birth parents, or those who had ongoing contact but had not established a relationship of warmth and trust. Some of the latter group described situations which would suggest that these were birth parents who had not been able to adjust to the loss of their child through adoption, despite continuing contact.

Given that some of the placements had been made in most difficult circumstances, the positive outcome for adoptive parents, and, in their view, for many of the birth parents, was a tribute to the generosity and understanding of both adoptive and birth parents.

Contrasts between those who were most positive and those least positive about openness

Although numbers were small, there did seem to be some common factors in the 16 families in which contact or links were viewed as generally positive and the six families in which reservations were expressed.

The most positive

There were 24 children for whom continued contact with birth parents, whether through links or face-to-face contact, was described as beneficial in relation to their needs. They were a disparate group, ranging in age at placement from two weeks to 14 years, although only three (excluding those with learning difficulties) were aged nine or more at placement. Characteristics associated with most positive placements were:

– the child feeling free to attach to the adoptive parents to an extent which they found rewarding. The adoptive parents felt the children were well integrated into the family

– the child being aware of the good relationship between the two sets of parents. Several of the adoptive parents commented they had found the birth parents to be more likeable or less difficult than the picture which had been conveyed by social workers (who had frequently been involved in adversarial situations with the birth parents)

– the adoptive parents believing that the child had been helped by contact to achieve a sense of identity and an understanding of the circumstances of her or his adoption

– the adoptive parents feeling that contact with birth parents was a means of providing continuity and, in at least four placements, the birth parent having helped the child to make the transition to the new family

– the birth parents being seen by the adoptive parents to be fulfilling an appropriate role, so that the child did not experience divided loyalties while still maintaining links with people important to her or him. The role adopted by birth parents was generally described as that of a non-parental relative such as an aunt or uncle or a more distant member of the family. Several of the adoptive parents described the relationship between the two families as being like that of an extended family network and, indeed, they would meet together at weddings, birthdays and other family celebrations

– the adoptive parents and birth parents negotiating an agreement directly and meetings taking place either in the home of the birth family or the adoptive family. No social workers were involved.

The least positive
There were several contrasting features between the placements of the 24 children in the 16 families who viewed openness positively and

those of eight children living in six families which were associated with some tension or difficulty. Generally, the children in this group had had more adverse experiences prior to placement. Six of the eight children had been separated from their birth parents many years earlier, some as long as ten years, before placement. They had then spent a lengthy period in residential care during which contact with birth parents had been irregular, unstructured and inconsistent. Further factors which appeared to be associated with the less marked success of openness were that:

- all these children had been seven years or more at placement and six had been nine years or older. It is known from other research studies that this age range is a difficult one in terms of children's ability to adjust and form attachments

- there was not a good relationship in these placements between the adoptive parents and the birth parents. In one case this was accounted for by the fact that the adoptive parents refused to meet the birth mother but, in five other placements, the birth parents had conveyed some sense of disapproval or unhappiness. There was therefore tension between the families, either currently or in the past

- in four of these six placements, the children met birth parents on neutral territory with a social worker present. It is not clear whether this contributed to the poor development of the relationship between adoptive and birth parents or whether it was a necessary arrangement because of the tension

- the birth parents of six of these eight children had conveyed disapproval of the adoption plan and had given agreement only at a very late stage or, in one case, had withheld agreement. Two birth mothers were described as having burdened the child with their own loss and sadness and were thought not to have relinquished the parental role, in that they viewed continuing contact as a possible route to restoration

- all the children had experienced some early deprivation or abuse.

It would be relevant to consider the placements of these eight children alongside research findings about difficulties in placing older children in the UK, especially those with a long history of residential care. Hill et al[10] reported that about one-third of the 50 adoptive and permanent foster families in their study in Scotland 'regarded the child's attachment as less than they had hoped for'. Thoburn et al[11] found that children needing contact with birth parents were less likely to be attached to new families whether they had contact or not. And in their summary of the survey through which some of the children in this study were identified, Fratter et al[12] stated that age was 'the only factor which seems clearly and consistently associated with breakdown'. For children aged eight at placement the breakdown rate was 23 per cent and it increased to 40 per cent for children aged 12 to 14. But, while acknowledging that the placements of younger children in this study with contact seemed the least problematic, it must not be overlooked that there were three boys, placed at ages nine, 13 and 14 respectively, whose adoptive parents felt that adoption with contact had worked well. However, these three boys had had fewer identified problems at placement than those adopted by the six families who had described difficulties and, furthermore, their birth parents had been supportive of the plan for adoption.

Concluding comments

Limitations of the study
There are a number of limitations to this study in terms of generalising from the sample of adoptive parents and adopted children:

- the small number of families involved does not provide scope for statistical analysis

- the sample was likely to have been biased in that all the adoptive parents had either agreed or volunteered to take part. Therefore, at the very least, they all felt comfortable in discussing adoption and many indicated that their willingness to be interviewed derived from their positive feelings about open adoption. There is no way of assessing how far the attitude of the adoptive parents interviewed was typical of adoptive parents generally

- there may have been a tendency for the adoptive parents to diminish their sense of discomfort and dissatisfaction, either in order to justify the type of adoption in which they were involved or to respond positively to what was clearly an area of interest to the researcher

- the picture conveyed by the adoptive parents was essentially a 'snapshop' revealing how openness felt at the time of the interview. The impact on their adopted children was important to all the parents and, as only two children had by then reached adulthood, views about benefits and disadvantages could change over time. The study by Rowe et al[13] of children in long-term foster care showed that children's feelings about contact with birth parents fluctuated and this is also recognised in the children of divorced parents. It is likely, therefore, that at various stages in the placement adoptive parents' assessment of the importance to children of contact with birth parents would be different. In addition, children are more or less aware of their adoptive status at different stages and their feelings about its significance will not be constant

- this evaluation of the adoptive placements is based on the perspective of the adoptive parents only and the other important parties, children and birth parents, were not asked to offer their views

- the majority of placements (those in 16 families) were made by voluntary agencies whereas most placements in the UK are now undertaken by local authorities.

Indications for future practice
Despite the note of caution about the scope of this exploratory study, when placed alongside the studies available on open adoption from New Zealand and the USA, together with UK studies about the placements of children with special needs,[14] it can identify some useful directions for future practice.

Selection and preparation of adoptive parents
The study confirms the findings of those in New Zealand and in the USA about the impact of agency policy and attitudes on both adoptive parents and birth parents. It is clear that, at present in the UK, the possibility of any degree of openness being offered to birth parents and adoptive parents will depend on which agency they approach. As the development of openness is linked with agency attitudes, and

these in turn influence adoptive parents, there may be adoptive parents who are implicitly encouraged to 'reject the difference' and deny the significance of the birth family to their adopted child. Agencies in the past may have underestimated the potential of adoptive parents to develop an openness of attitude because of prevailing views about the necessity for a 'clean break'. In addition, there may be a reluctance on the part of social workers to relinquish some of the power and control conferred by the closed adoption model. Agencies which believed in the value of maintaining links with a child's family of origin were successful in making placements where children's links were not severed.

The study demonstrates that adoptive parents who are willing to maintain links or contact after adoption *can* be found, provided that agencies can offer the necessary counselling and preparation. The openness of attitude with which adoptive parents embarked on the placements in the study was significant, in that an open attitude can maximise the benefits for themselves and for the child of even limited contact with birth parents. Openness of attitude on the part of adoptive parents did not guarantee that they would experience an open adoption as satisfying, but it did seem to be a pre-requisite of enhancing the benefits of contact for the child. This was particularly so with face-to-face contact, although openness of attitude is important in all placements. The selection and preparation of adoptive parents by agencies needs to take into account their potential to develop openness of attitude.

It was the experience of the agencies in the study that contact with birth relatives other than parents raised similar issues for adoptive parents. However, with less potential role conflict, contact with non-parental relatives was seen as more straightforward and sometimes its complexities were underestimated. Some adoptive parents could feel threatened by any link with birth relatives, however limited the threat was in reality in terms of role conflict. The same careful selection and preparation processes should apply, whatever contact is proposed.

Alternatives to the closed adoption model can certainly assist adoptive parents in their complex task. In 1971, Jane Rowe urged social workers to develop a clearer understanding of the realities of adoption and the adoptive relationship, in order to assist adoptive parents to deal with the

> double bind of 'make this child your own but tell him he isn't'.
> Adopters must be helped to integrate the child and yet to provide
> him [or her] with a vivid, lasting and acceptable picture of the
> natural parents. The bare facts are not enough, even if all the facts
> were available which usually they are not. Adopters need to feel
> some kind of kinship with the people who gave 'their' child birth.
> They need to understand, and to accept, to incorporate the child's
> antecedents into their family.[15]

It seemed to the researcher that at least half of the adoptive parents
in the study had been able to achieve this sense of 'kinship' through
contact. Social workers can help other adopters to do the same.

Work with birth parents

The study highlighted ways in which birth parents can contribute
positively, both before and after adoption, by conveying to the
adoptive parents and to the children their acceptance of the plan for
adoption, and by maintaining an appropriate role. It is essential that
agencies help to prepare birth parents for their changed role and
relationship.

What little experience there was in the study of birth parents'
involvement in the choice of adoptive parents – now the norm in New
Zealand – suggests that this is also a practice which agencies here
should consider offering in appropriate cases. This is likely to be able
to be arranged relatively easily where adoptive parents are sought for
infants and toddlers being relinquished voluntarily. There are likely to
be fewer families available when older children or those with special
needs are being placed. Even so, there are considerable gains to all
parties if birth parents can participate in the choice of an adoptive
family.

Age of child at placement

The number of children placed under the age of five who were having
face-to-face contact with birth parents was unexpected but they, and
all but two of the children placed under the age of nine, were
described as experiencing no difficulties with contact. Adoptive
parents had found that their children *could* make an attachment to
two sets of parents.

The placement of children and young people over the age of nine tended to be more complex, mainly as a result of the children's difficulties of adjustment and yet this is the age group of children for whom open adoption is most often suggested. Certainly open adoption is no panacea for the unresolved feelings of children and birth parents and social workers should not attempt to use it as such. Overall, however, the positive results of this study may be considered to be reassuring.

Degrees of openness

The maintenance of communication between the families after adoption, whether directly or via the agency, can be of benefit in the short term. In addition, it keeps the door open for a meeting to take place at any later time when this may be seen as helpful to the child. This happened in three instances in the present study where adoptive parents themselves had initiated contact.

Meetings between birth parents and adoptive parents, especially when they occurred before placement and following counselling and preparation, were very much welcomed. Agency workers and adoptive parents both described how adoptive parents and birth parents benefited directly, while children benefited directly or indirectly depending on their age and degree of understanding.

The feelings of adoptive parents and of some adoption agencies about *continuing* face-to-face contact after adoption were more mixed, although the majority of adoptive parents in the study felt that their children had gained in a number of important ways from meetings and there were many examples of particularly successful open adoption placements of this sort. For six children, ongoing contact had been a prerequisite of their giving agreement to being adopted.

Final thoughts

Open adoption in which children continue to maintain contact with birth parents represents a major departure from the traditional concept of adoption in the UK. In particular, it acknowledges the continuing significance to children of their birth parents and the potential of children to maintain some form of attachment to biological as well as psychological parents. The recognition of the appropriateness of open adoption for some children can usefully be compared with studies about children in divorce. In the same way that contact with birth parents after adoption contradicts the extreme position of some advocates of permanency over whether or not links should be severed, so findings in research into divorce about 'the centrality of both parents to the psychological health of children and adolescents alike'[16] offer a view diametrically opposed to the 'clean break' approach advocated by Goldstein, Freud and Solnit.[17]

Further research about the impact of openness on the adopted person will need to be undertaken before an assessment can be made of its value in the longer term. There is insufficient evidence from this or other studies in the UK to date to indicate that a form of open adoption in which birth parents continue to have face-to-face contact after adoption should become the norm. However, the experience of the wide range of voluntary agencies and adoptive parents interviewed in this study and their generally positive feelings about greater openness in adoption suggest that voluntary and statutory agencies could usefully be exploring the development of alternatives to the closed adoption model. Present legislation and case law provide a framework in which this can be done. Furthermore, the Government's inter-departmental proposals for change, which are at a consultative stage at the time of writing, indicate an irreversible trend in that direction.

The study reported here demonstrates that a child's need for contact does not necessarily conflict with the achievement of permanence. The experience of agencies which have developed greater openness in adoption and of the adoptive parents in the study demonstrates that alternatives to the closed adoption model – although more complex for the participants and more demanding of the agency – can enrich the lives of the adopted children, their birth parents and their birth relatives.

References

1   Fratter J *Family placement and access: achieving permanency for children in contact with birth parents* Barnardo's, 1989.

2   Fratter J, Rowe J, Sapsford D and Thoburn J *Permanent family placement: a decade of experience* BAAF, 1991.

3   Howell D and Ryburn M 'New Zealand: new ways to choose adopters' *Adoption & Fostering* 11 4, 1987.

4   See 2 above.

5   Packman J, Randall J and Jacques N *Who needs care? Social work decisions about children* Blackwell, 1986.
    Richards MPM 'Behind the best interests of the child: an examination of the arguments of Goldstein, Freud and Solnit concerning custody and access at divorce' *Journal of social welfare law*, March 1986.
    Rillera MJ and Kaplan S *Co-operative adoption: a handbook* Westminster, Ca: Triadoption Publications, 1985.

6   Millham S, Bullock R, Hosie K and Haak M *Lost in care: the problems of maintaining links between children in care and their families* Gower, 1986.

7   Triseliotis J 'Adoption with contact' *Adoption & Fostering* 9 4, 1985.

8   Thoburn J, Murdock A and O'Brian A *Permanence in child care* Blackwell, 1986.

9   Houghton Committee *Report of the departmental committee on the adoption of children* Cmd 5107, HMSO, 1972.

10 Hill M, Hutton S and Easton S 'Adoptive parenting – plus and minus' *Adoption & Fostering* 12 2, 1988.

11 See 8 above.

12 See 2 above.

13 Rowe J, Cain H, Hundleby M and Keane A *Long-term foster care* Batsford/BAAF, 1984.

14 Wedge P and Thoburn J (eds) *Finding families for 'hard-to-place' children* BAAF, 1986.
    Rushton A, Treseder J and Quinton D *New parents for older children* BAAF, 1988.
    See also 10 above.

15 Rowe J 'The reality of the adoptive family' in Tod RJN (ed) *Social work in adoption* Longman, 1971.

16 Wallerstein J and Kelly J *Surviving the break-up* New York: Basic Books/ Grant McIntyre, 1980.

17 Goldstein J, Freud A and Solnit AJ *Beyond the best interests of the child* New York: Free Press of Glencoe, 1973.
    Goldstein J, Freud A and Solnit AJ *Before the best interests of the child* Burnett Books/Andre Deutsch, 1980.

3 Openness and adoptive parents

Murray Ryburn

Defining openness

Traditionally, Western adoption is located both in economic motivations – to transfer the care of children from the public to the private purse – and in paternalistic convictions about the role of the state in family life. In the latter, through the legislature, the judiciary and professionals with mandated powers such as social workers, the state protects and promotes what are regarded as the best interests of those seen as unwilling or incapable of making decisions about these things for themselves. Those for whom such decisions are made in adoption have been deemed unentitled or incapable of exercising a proper voice. In the case of adopted people, this has been by virtue of their age while, in the case of birth parents, it has often been by virtue of perceived lack of parenting capacity, personality characteristics, degree of maturity, behaviour, and so on. Prospective adoptive parents have had judgements made about them in the same kind of way and on some of the same criteria. The problem for all members of the adoption triangle is that, however well intentioned the decisions made about them may be, there has usually been minimal consultation with them.

In reaction to this, openness in adoption is perhaps most usefully seen, not in terms purely of policy and practice, but rather as a set of ideas and beliefs. These have their origins in the attempts of some consumers and adoption professionals to rechannel the traditional flow of power in twentieth century Western adoption. They hold a central belief in the maintenance of some degree of contact in adoption and the maximum of consumer control over the process. They see these as having, for all parties, significant advantages over a system that is led by professionals and based on the customary severance of all contact between birth families and adopting families. Openness, in this context, represents an ideological commitment which affords an antidote to the belief that professionals 'know best'.

The central challenge for social workers and practitioners in adoption, who resist the pull to collude in the belief that they can necessarily determine the best interests of others, is to find a way to restore to adoption consumers full rights to participation in the discourse about their own lives and futures.

Attempts to do so are often hampered by two things. First, by a failure to take full account of the fact that adoption is both for the present and for the future, so that decisions taken in the light of present knowledge and understanding require the flexibility to accommodate changing future circumstances. They need to reflect the fact, for example, that someone who has no clear voice at the age of one or two, *will* have opinions by the time they are ten or eleven, and very strong views indeed by 20, 40 and 70. Similarly, someone who fails to discharge their parenting responsibilities to what is considered a good enough standard at the age of 19 or 20, could have much to offer as a parent by 30 or 40. On the other hand, someone who seems confident and competent to parent someone else's infant at 30 or 35 may be racked with doubt and uncertainty in parenting the now adolescent child when they reach 45 or 50. And the adoptive parents who accept that their child already has a history on joining their family, could later feel overwhelmed by that self-same history.

The second obstacle to according partnership in decision-making to consumers is the common view that openness in adoption only has advantages to offer to birth parents, and that gains for the other parties are minimal. Allied to this is a belief that there is unlikely to be any way of managing adoptions which could best serve the interests of all parties, that the interests of the parties have to be viewed separately, and that in these circumstances the perceived interests of children should predominate.

Openness in adoption constitutes a way to empower adoption consumers. It has the distinct advantage that, unlike the law which represents an attempt to 'freeze time', it allows for continuing negotiation for changing future circumstances. It has significant advantages to offer all the parties to adoption: birth families, adopting families, and children and young people who are to be adopted. This paper will focus in particular on the advantages it can offer to adoptive parents, often regarded as those who have the least to gain from openness,[1] and will draw in part on experience gained through adoption practice in New Zealand.

Defining contact: an evolutionary model

It is important at the outset to distinguish between openness in adoption, on the one hand, and access, on the other, since the concepts are different but often confused. Access is a term that has come to us from private family law. It derives from a value system in which parents are viewed as having rights over their children. One of those rights, when there has been divorce or separation or where children are in substitute care, is that of a parent or parents to see their child and therefore to have 'access' to them. There is no sense of mutuality in the term, which describes a one-way transaction based on an application by the parent. The parameters of any meetings between parents and children are firmly delineated. The 1989 Children Act brings a welcome change in introducing the term 'contact'. This term implies two-way relationships, which children can also initiate, where face-to-face meetings are not the only means of establishing and maintaining links. Possibilities for contact will also extend beyond the bounds of child-parent, parent-child relationships. The capacity for such contact to be regulated in law, however, will still distinguish it from the sorts of relationships to be found in open adoption.

Openness in adoption – the maintenance of some degree of contact between all the parties: birth parents, adoptive parents, and children and young people – is very far removed from the concept of access. It is not defined in law and indeed the law, whilst not prohibiting it, in general discourages contact through, for example, the restrictive provisions relating to the confidentiality of birth records. Many practitioners of openness in adoption argue, in fact, that it is not possible to regulate human relationships by law, and that openness depends for its success not on legal regulation but on a conviction by all parties that it is the most effective way of managing relationships in adoption.

The contact between the parties to an adoption, where there is openness, may take many forms. It may range from the occasional exchange of letters and cards via an agency to more direct contact by telephone, or face-to-face meetings in which an intermediary is no longer necessary. Within this wide range, there will also naturally be wide variation in the frequency and duration of contact, ranging perhaps from annual contact by post to something which is much more akin to shared parenting.

It is important to stress that this contact, when there is openness, is evolutionary in the way that any relationship is. The initial contact that the parties may agree on can be vastly different from the contact that may develop over time. Relationships in open adoption are thus continuously renegotiated, like any other relationships, though the general trend is usually from formal or semi-formal contact to much more informal contact in which the facilitation of an agency is no longer necessary.

The contact between Annie and her birth mother Andrea offers a good example. There was an initial meeting between all of the parties at the time of placement, and there followed several years of contact by letter. The adoptive parents sent Andrea regular letters updating her on Annie's progress and also photographs of Annie and her family. They would always send letters at milestones such as Annie's birthday, or at Christmas time, but they sent many other letters which did not necessarily relate to any special event in Annie's life. Andrea also sent regular letters to Annie and her family informing them of changes and developments in her life. As Annie grew up she would also draw pictures and make things for Andrea which would be posted to her. At this point in their relationship, all of the letter contact was via the agency that arranged the original placement.

When Annie was five years old, Andrea decided that she felt confident and comfortable enough with the idea of meeting Annie and her family and asked the agency to make this request for her. Annie's adoptive parents welcomed the contact. Initially Annie and her mother met Andrea at a neutral setting and then subsequently the whole family met Andrea and her boyfriend. After that time, there developed informal contact which the parties negotiated directly. There would be telephone contact which could be initiated by Annie, Andrea, or Lynne and Lindsay, the adoptive parents. There were always meetings at Christmas time and birthdays, and in between there would be other informal contact at least once a month.

When Annie reached seven or eight, the contact to some extent diminished, and this seemed to suit the needs of both Annie and Andrea. Andrea, at this point in her life, had entered a new relationship and had also begun a new job and Annie, like many children of her age, was beginning to become much more pre-occupied with her own internal world. There continued to be regular contact at main events like Christmas and birthdays and phone contact at other times, with occasional informal meetings. It is likely that when Annie reaches adolescence and begins, like all teenagers, to develop a clearer sense of her own identity, her relationship with her birth mother will assume a greater importance and there is likely to be another increase in the level of contact.

The striking thing about this sort of relationship, which is not atypical of arrangements where there is openness in adoption, is that it quite clearly does not lend itself to regulation by the courts or to stipulation in a formal agreement by the parties. It takes account of constantly changing relationships and circumstances and ultimately permits adopted people themselves a major voice in the key relationships in their lives.

A sense of 'entitlement' for adopters through severance of contact
The tradition since the passing of the first adoption legislation in England and Wales in 1926 has been for the complete severance of contact between birth families and adopting families. This tradition was summed up at an adoption hearing in 1965 when a judge said:

> In general, it is the policy of the law to make the veil between the past and present lives of adopted persons as opaque and impenetrable as possible, like the veil which God has placed between the living and the dead.[2]

Chilling though these words may sound, the drawing of such a veil between a child or young person and their family of origin is often still a key aim of adoption policy and practice.

Adoptive parents have usually been seen as having the most to lose if there is not a complete severance of contact. As this adoptive parent described to me, speaking of the adoption of a daughter some 25 years before:

> We were encouraged to go back home and live our lives as if she has been born to us – that would be best for us and best for her. It was crucial for the welfare of all of us, we believed and we were told, to make her ours in every way. If insecurity stepped in, it could destroy everything we were trying to create.

Such a fear found its expression in many ways. One of the more striking was a new vocabulary. There was from the 1960s, for example, the use of words like 'entitlement' and 'claiming' to describe the need for adopting parents to attach to their children in order to create the conditions for security and success in placement. The fact that a much more commonly used term, 'attachment' – which has implications for a reciprocal relationship – should be replaced by words like 'claim' and 'entitle', which seem to relate more to a legal or property domain than they do to human relationships, is significant. It implies a need, born of fear, for adoptive families to establish themselves to the exclusion of birth families.

These words – used, of course, by professionals in adoption rather than adoptive parents – serve also to illustrate that children have continued to be viewed in a proprietorial way. The entitlement works all in one direction. No account it taken of what the future 'entitlement' of children and young people should be, in terms of having some choice about the relationships they would want with other significant people in their lives. It was believed that, if their adoptive parents were helped to feel unchallenged in their role, this would work to the best advantage of the children also. What we have slowly been discovering over the years, however, is that those whom such practices sought to protect and to make secure in their new families – adopted people – are beginning to say that they do not wish for, and would never have wanted, this sort of protection. Birth parents, too, are beginning to end their silent diffidence in order to let us know that they cannot, and would never wish to, forget the child they lost through adoption.

Security to parent threatened by knowledge of the past?
There was a contradictory development in adoption in the 1960s and 1970s which existed in uneasy relationship with concepts like entitlement and claiming. This was the idea developed through the work of Erik Erikson[3] and John Triseliotis,[4] that access for adopted people to knowledge and information about the past was essential to the development of a healthy sense of personal identity in the present and for the future. Adoption practice began to alter. It changed from a positive encouragement to adoptive parents *not* to reveal to their child much, if anything, about their origins for fear of damaging family security, to an approach where it was seen as important for children to know something about their adoptive status. A dilemma was thus posed. Adoptive parents were now in the position of having to parent their children as if in every sense they were their own, whilst

bringing them up with the sure knowledge that they had not been born to them. This is a dilemma still faced by countless adoptive parents today. It is a dilemma born of the fear that contact will damage security and attachment.

More than 25 years ago, David Kirk[5] maintained that the success or failure of adoptive parenting could depend on the capacity of adoptive parents to distinguish the difference between parenting by adoption and parenting by birth. Few workers and consumers in adoption would doubt the wisdom of Kirk's thesis. However, the difficulties inherent in accepting such role difference where there is no contact with birth families can be enormous. One adoptive mother whose daughters, now in their late twenties, made contact with their birth families when they were in their teens, explained her uneasiness:

> When I met Lorraine (the birth mother of Christine, one of her daughters), I felt threatened. It's silly now, when I think about it, but I did feel really threatened and I felt that maybe Christine would think more of Lorraine than she did of me, and it was hard to define my feelings. It was just that I felt, well, not exactly disappointed, but I felt that I was, in myself, if I was honest, just as much of a mother to Christine so that she was like my very own flesh and blood. It was very hard to take. It's different now. I mean, no children really are *yours* – you don't own them. But meeting Lorraine meant that I had to admit the fact that there was somebody else there for the first time in my life.

Although adoptive parents often talk of facing continuing reminders that their children were not born to them, confidently acknowledging the difference between birth and adoptive parenting is very difficult, as it had been over the years for Evelyn, the adoptive parent quoted above. The adoptive parent below described it very well:

> You see we were very naive in thinking that, in fact, an adoptive relationship can be the same as a natural relationship. It can't be, but I don't see that it is any less valid because of that. We wanted the door closed when the children were young – what we were aiming for was a family as much like others as possible. But when Lucy was about ten or so, there was an awful lot of exposure on television and so on, and gradually the whole climate of opinion changed and we changed with it. I came to see that really we were basing something on a pretence which we didn't need. It wasn't

necessary to pretend that this was like every other family. This was *our family* and it happened to be set up by adoption, and to me that was valid and my feelings were just as strong as other parents'. Maybe different, but just as strong.

Only some degree of openness and continuing contact between adoptive families and birth families offers adoptive parents a ready way out of the dilemma of parenting their children exactly as if they were born to them, while at the same time helping them to understand that they were not.

The children of two sets of parents
Openness in adoption makes it possible for adopted children and young people to be who they really are: the children of two sets of parents. Neil, an adoptive parent who has regular contact with both the birth parents of his son Robin, described the growing advantage of such contact for him:

> I previously did think of Maria and Tom in an aunt and uncle role but I think that, as our contact grows, I do now think of us as the adoptive parents and them as the birth parents and it just feels very comfortable.

Many adoptive parents in open adoptions talk of the greater sense of security that comes to them from the sort of acknowledgment of difference that Neil highlights. Mary, an adoptive parent, commented:

> Because of the contact with Suzanne's birth mother and grandmother, James and I feel confirmed in our role as her parents. We were always very aware of how painful the placement decision had been for them and, through the contact that we now have with them, I think we feel much more secure knowing that they feel good about us as Suzanne's parents.

An adoptive parent, who had no contact with either of her children's birth parents, spoke of a contrasting experience.

> I would have loved the chance to meet my children's birth parents. It would have been a sense of realism and I wouldn't have been left with fantasies ... I think meeting them would have made me stronger. I would have set limits much more easily and been more confident, and the kids would have benefited from that.

Whereas another adoptive parent with contact had this to say:

> Openness now means there aren't any secrets any more. I can just get on with being Sharon's mum and, because of the contact I have with Rachael (Sharon's birth mother), I know she feels good about me as Sharon's mum too.

Opponents of some form of continuing contact in adoption frequently state that children cannot sustain significant relationships with more than one set of parents. They maintain that continuing birth family contact will be confusing for children and will lessen their sense of attachment to their adoptive family. For many professionals in adoption, the origins of this idea lie in two books by Goldstein, Freud and Solnit, *Beyond the best interests of the child*,[6] and *Before the best interests of the child*.[7]

These writers' assertion that, when children have to be placed permanently in substitute care, the severance of past contacts is necessary in order for them to make a secure attachment to a new permanent family, was founded on their clinical experience and judgements and not on any empirical research. There has been a growing body of research since then which, without doubt, points in the opposite direction and indicates that children are capable both of forming new attachments[8] and of sustaining significant attachments with more than one set of parent figures.[9]

This debate is, in any case, something of an irrelevance in open adoption, since it confuses the status of *being a parent* with the activity of *parenting*. As one adoptive parent, whose teenage daughter has had contact with her birth mother over the past eight years, said to me very recently, 'Marcia will always be her birth mother but I'm the one who does the mothering.'

Children are very well aware of who their parents are. Their parents are the ones who get them up in the morning, get them dressed, get them breakfast, help get them off to school and collect them after school, put them to bed and read them bedtime stories. Nothing about openness in adoption diminishes the role of parenthood for adoptive parents, and to suggest that it does is to apply a muddled form of adult thinking to a child's world. Nor, of course, is love a finite resource, diminished in proportion to the number of loving relationships which we have.

There is ample evidence from studies in divorce and separation to indicate, furthermore, that children are able to negotiate complex relationships even when they have multiple parenting figures.[10] The significant fact seems to be whether there is a relationship devoid of major conflict between the adult parties.[11] When I raised the question of whether an open placement was likely to be confusing with one adoptive father whose two children have continuing contact with their birth families, he remarked:

> It's never occurred to me as confusing – maybe more complicated. I don't think it's a thing that does confuse children. Children accept established relationships the way they are. That's why we haven't felt threatened at all, because we are well established as their mother and father in our house.

Another adoptive parent whose child has continuing contact with both extended birth families concurs:

> It seems to be just such a natural thing. If it's not confusing for us, I don't think it will be confusing for him. It's just a fact of life. It's just the way it's going to be, and I think he will grow up just accepting it the way we do.

An eight-year-old described to me in an interview how, though some of the boys in her class may have confusing ideas about openness in adoption, she herself takes the idea of having two mothers in her stride:

> Some of the boys in our class don't even know what adopted means. They say to me that I'm adopted and they say to me that I'm stupid because they think I've got three or four mothers but I've only got two. Some of the people that are in our class are adopted and haven't met their birth mothers yet and they say that I'm really lucky because I have, and I just say to the boys to be quiet about it. I tell them it's really good. I'm really lucky to have two mothers and two fathers as well.

Her older brother, who had not then been able to establish contact with his birth family, observed how it was much easier for her to have contact because it was something she had grown up with, whereas for him, at 13, 'it would be pretty hard because I wouldn't know what to say'. Nevertheless, he has since gone on to cope successfully with establishing contact with his birth mother, despite his normal teenage shyness and reserve.

Answering the questions

Another significant advantage of openness for adoptive parents is that it is much easier for them to answer their children's questions as they grow. As children, we always expect our parents to have all of the answers – indeed, it is a salutary moment for many of us when we realise that they may no more have the answers than we do ourselves! Such a belief, however, for children helps them to create a safe environment in which to test out relationships and to explore the world. Children's requests for information about their past and where they come from are not predictable. For different children they will come at different times and often in the most difficult circumstances.

> Of course, you always imagine yourself talking to your child about this in the cosiest possible circumstances. You are sitting by the fire in the evening, and you've had a lovely read, and you've talked and cuddled, and they say ' Mummy . . .' and you give them all the right answers at the right time whereas, in fact, Martin was driving a carload of children to the cinema, and it was pouring wet, a cold winter day, and the car was all steamed up, and all of a sudden Lucy bawled out, 'Why did my real mother not want me, Daddy?' He was trying to make a difficult turn at the time, and he said he came out in a sweat.

It is just not possible to predict all of an adopted child or young person's need for information about their past as they grow up. Although there has been an improvement in recent years in the sort of information that is given at the time of placement to parents who adopt (though often still not to birth families), what children will need to know as they grow up may often not even be articulated. Where there is continuing contact, many of these questions can simply be answered, often without the need for the question ever to be asked. Where there is not openness in adoption, adoptive parents may often face questions that they are unable to answer. It is certainly possible that when adoptive parents are unable to satisfy their children's need to know about their history, the trust upon which a child's sense of security is founded could be threatened.

In interviewing Richard, for example, aged 34, shortly after he had been reunited with his birth mother, it became apparent that one of the most significant questions he would have liked an answer to as he grew up was whether or not his mother had an interest in 'restoring old things'. It would seem that, as Richard grew up, he developed a hobby of collecting old junk – toys and the like – and restoring them. Reading between the lines of my interview with him, it seemed that he was often ostracised by other children who thought his hobby rather strange. It was with an overwhelming sense of relief that he discovered that his birth mother, Sue, also liked to collect and to restore old things. The effect of learning the answer to this question, and others, for Richard meant that 'I suddenly felt normal . . . you know, sort of good, as though you were just part of the human race again.' It would have taken an extremely perceptive social worker at the time of placement to recognise that one of Richard's greatest information needs as he grew up would be for him to know that his mother, like him, enjoyed collecting and restoring second-hand objects.

The identity issues that can trouble some children and young people growing up in adoptive families were highlighted in an article many years ago by H J Sants.[12] Sants uses the metaphor of the Hans Christian Andersen fairytale *The ugly duckling* to describe this problem. The ugly duckling, as Sants reminds us, was a swan who had the misfortune to be born in a duck's yard. A succession of well-intended substitute parents, including a cat and a rooster, tried unsuccessfully to parent the ugly duckling and give her a sense of who she was. However, it was not until one day, as she sailed down the river and encountered a wondrous creature who looked just like her, that the ugly duckling's identity problems were over and she realised that she was, in fact, a swan. In her case, and in the case of some people who are adopted, only seeing can be believing.

Sharing the satisfactions

Adoptive families who have continuing contact with their children's birth families also comment on how important it is to them to be able to share with someone else – to whom the child means a great deal – the joys, pleasures, and satisfactions of parenting. All parents enjoy recounting the gains, changes and developments their children make but it adds an additional quality for adoptive parents to share these things with the birth families of their children, for whom they will also hold an intense and special interest.

Adoptive parents also talk, where there is openness in adoption, about having a yardstick for measuring the progress and development of their child, or for offering them clues to help them understand their child's personality.

> I just became more and more aware that Deborah wasn't like us and didn't have our personalities or interests. I used to hate the family gatherings where everyone would talk about children. You know: 'He's just like his dad, *he* was late walking' and so on. I just felt so aware that I didn't know about Deb's parents. I didn't know what to expect.

Adoptive parents who have continuing contact with the birth families of their children often speak about having more realistic expectations for their children as a consequence. One adoptive parent put it like this:

> Because of the contact we have, and because we know all about them – medical history, cultural background – I'm sure that we've been more free in letting them be brought up not like ourselves.

An adoptive parent of a child with severe learning difficulties spoke to me recently about the great satisfaction she has gained from some of her daughter's achievements. Measured against the yardstick of normal development such achievements would go largely unnoticed. For *her* child, however, the achievement of finally learning to use a spoon to eat was an immense milestone, even though it went mostly unacknowledged by other people. To her, the opportunity to share this with one of her child's birth parents was immensely important and more than compensated for the failure of many friends, even her own immediate family, to take note of her daughter's achievement.

Positive messages

It has long been recognised by workers in adoption that it is vital for children and young people who are adopted to receive positive messages about their past and their family of origin as they grow up.[13] Many adopted people describe having had to face the dilemma of believing either that they were so bad their birth families did not want to keep them, or that their birth families were so bad they didn't care about them enough to do so. In either case, it is very difficult for them to have positive feelings about their origins, and some describe the harmful effect this has had on their sense of self-worth and self-esteem. Adoptive parents in these situations also feel that they are inevitably classed in the 'good' role – as the rescuer of their child – and this is uncomfortable and difficult for them as well. In the absence of any contact with birth families, it can sometimes be extremely difficult for parents by adoption to have anything other than a very negative view of their child's birth family, especially when abuse or neglect has been the reason for the child's placement for adoption.

There are, of course, very few parents who do not love their children and want the best for them. Even parents who abuse their children usually love them but are often trapped in an escalating spiral of difficulties, exacerbated by things like poverty and the lack of any good parental role-modelling in their own childhoods. For these parents, often the problems may be that they do not love their children in the right sorts of ways. For adoptive parents to have contact with such birth families can be vital in allowing them to develop views of their child's birth family which are not entirely bad.

All of us have good qualities and no one ever deserves to be written off as a parent as if they had nothing to offer. Sadly, very often where there are contested adoptions, the only images that prospective adoptive parents have of birth families are the negative ones created in an adversarial court setting. And birth parents, naturally enough, when they believe that adoption will mean the total severance of all contact with their child, are much more likely to behave in extreme ways which only add credence to a totally dismissive view of them. These are the parents who, as the Dartington researchers commented,[14] will have sat and failed a 'love-test' which was 'set and marked by social workers' and for which they were 'ill-prepared and without a syllabus'. When adoptive parents have contact with these birth families, they can often add to their picture of them a new understanding born of first-hand knowledge and an awareness of the terrible deprivations or the tremendous stresses under which they must live their lives.

A shift in the attitude of adoptive parents, as a consequence of the opportunity for contact, can also lead to new and different behaviour on behalf of birth parents and birth families. I have known several situations where birth parents, having had the opportunity for some contact with prospective adoptive families and having through that contact helped to accomplish a change in the attitudes of the adoptive families towards them, have gone on to share information. They have even prepared family history material for their birth children in situations where they had, in the past, absolutely refused to participate in any way in placement plans for their children. The research of Joan Fratter[15] is instructive here. The possibilities for some form of continuing contact can mean that an adoption need not be contested in the courts and that birth parents find, instead, a positive role to play in their children's lives.

Information for adoptive parents about the families of their children, where there has been conflict and the adoption has been contested, will inevitably be jaundiced if it is given in the absence of any direct contact. The images they have will have been filtered through a court battle in which the key object is to 'win', so that often the only version of truth they will hear about birth families is an essentially negative one. Where there is openness, on the other hand, as this birth mother remarked:

> It gives me comfort in that I can imagine her with them. In my mind, I can picture their family life because I know them, and they've met me and they know that I'm not some kind of ogre either. So they are not going to turn round to her and say: 'Your mother must have been disgusting and it's coming out in you.'

Adoptive parents often describe a belief that they need somehow to be better parents than anyone else. They are often acutely aware that they are parenting someone else's child and, where they feel cast in the role of rescuing a child because of the alleged behaviour of their child's birth family, this feeling is reinforced. Contact allows adoptive parents to see birth families as real people with their own hopes, aspirations and dreams for their child.

The traditional process by which adoptive parents are assessed, with its pass or fail punctuation, can be seen as encouraging the perception both of themselves and of birth families as either good or bad. Reforming the process of assessment in adoption (which a colleague and I have described elsewhere),[16] so that prospective adopters become participants in an education process which empowers them to make their own decisions, goes hand in hand with, and seems to encourage, an openness in adopters towards birth families. Perhaps, by being freed from an inherently judgmental process themselves, they are freed in turn to see birth families in ways that are less judgmental.

Even where it may not seem safe for children and young people to have direct contact with their birth parents because of abuse they have suffered, other forms of contact may be reasonable, and often there will be other people within the extended family who could continue to play a positive role in the life of the child or young person. Jane Rowe in her research, for example, found that contact for children in substitute care with their birth grandparents was almost universally positive and to be welcomed.[17] One of the things that adoptive parents describe where there is openness is the pleasure that can come from establishing relationships with a range of people in the extended birth family. As this adoptive mother described:

> Initially you only probably think about a birth mother but it mustn't stop at that. It goes right out. And Selina is really lucky because she's got aunties and an uncle, and she's got a birth Nanna who just absolutely loves her which is absolutely terrific because now she's got three Nannas, not two.

Conclusion

Openness in adoption has significant advantages to offer all parties. The advantages that it brings to adoptive parents are those that have probably received least attention. This is doubtless due to the fact that openness has traditionally been perceived as most threatening to adoptive parents and they have been regarded as the ones with the most to lose. On the contrary, however, adoption with openness leaves many adopters feeling more confirmed in their role of parenting someone else's child. It clarifies the distinction between being a parent and parenting, so that the roles of birth and adoptive parents are clear and more readily accepted. Openness makes it easier for adoptive parents to see that their children have the information they need as they grow up, and at the time which is right for them. It provides them with additional ways to measure the progress and development of their children, and it can be a potent force in combating the negative images of their children's birth families which an adversarial court system often creates.

Openness in adoption may sometimes seem to make life more complicated for its consumers. This is only because it makes explicit the factors and forces which always operate implicity, but less obviously, in closed adoptions. The result is that decisions and choices can be made on the basis of fuller knowledge. The act of making open what may otherwise be hidden offers also a means to challenge the concentration of power in professional hands in traditional Western adoption since it begins to afford the parties to adoption a voice in the discourse about *their* own lives. The relationships that can grow, develop and change in open adoptions may be so far removed from the legal fiction[18] that first created adoption in England and Wales in 1926, that at best the law may seem an irrelevance.

Successful human relationships are not prescribed in law or delineated in the courts – they are founded on trust and goodwill, and negotiated constantly over time through changing circumstances. The decision to sever contact between adoptive and birth families derives at base from a negative impulse – from fear and a perceived need to protect. There are, however, different ways to manage the difficult decisions that adoption brings, and openness – where the parties to adoption establish by negotiation the level of contact that seems right to them – places adoption on a similar footing to all of life's other significant relationships.

References

1   Rockel J and Ryburn M *Adoption today: change and choice in New Zealand* Auckland: Heinemann Reed, 1988.

2   Griffith K *Adoption: procedure, documentation and statistics. New Zealand 1881-1981* Wellington, published by the author, 1981.

3   Erikson E *Identity: youth and crisis* Faber, 1968.

4   Triseliotis J *In search of origins* Routledge & Kegan Paul, 1973.

5   Kirk D *Shared fate: a theory of adoption and mental health* Collier Macmillan, 1964.

6   Goldstein J. Freud A and Solnit A *Beyond the best interests of the child* New York: Free Press, 1973.

7   Goldstein J. Freud A and Solnit A *Before the best interests of the child* Burnett Books/André Deutsch, 1980.

8   Tizard B *Adoption: a second chance* Open Books, 1977.

9   See for example Schaffer R *Mothering* Fontana/Open Books, 1977; Thoburn J, Murdock A and O'Brien A *Permanence in child care* Blackwell, 1986; Thoburn J *Success and failure in permanent placement*

Avebury Gower, 1990; Fratter J *Family placement and access: achieving permanency for children in contact with birth parents* Barnardo's 1989.

10 Wallerstein J and Kelly J, *Surviving the break-up* New York: Grant MacIntyre, 1980.

11 See 10 above.

12 Sants H 'Genealogical bewilderment in children with substitute parents' *British Journal of Medical Psychology* 37, 1964.

13 See for example Triseliotis J 'Identity and security in adoption and long-term fostering' *Adoption & Fostering* 71, 1983.

14 Millham S, Bullock R, Hosie K and Little M *Lost in care: the problems of maintaining links between children in care and their families* Gower, 1986.

15 See 9 above.

16 Howell D and Ryburn M 'New Zealand: new ways to choose adopters' *Adoption & Fostering,* 11 4, 1987.

17 Rowe J, Cain H. Hundleby M and Keane A *Long-term foster care* Batsford/BAAF, 1984.

18 Adoption Act, 1926.

4 Transracial adoption – the most open adoption

Michael Mallows

In order to judge anything, we must ask ourselves what purpose it was intended to serve. Is adoption intended to meet the needs of the child or the parents (or even the professionals)? This question will have no single answer, of course, but it is a question that needs to be asked and adequately answered, whether discussing adoption in general or particular situations. Certainly, adoption in the UK is a very culturally-biased system. It is ethnocentric with a strong class bias (reflecting social work in general) and it has, for far too long, been yet another example of children being used primarily to serve the needs of adults. In the case of transracial adoption, there is an added dimension – exploitation – in that black babies and children, the most valuable resource a community has, have been taken away and denied knowledge about, information on, and contact with, that community. Whatever this does to the individual black parents, grandparents and other members of the extended family, it also hurts the wider community.

In other cultures, New Zealand Maori for example, children 'belong' not to separate parents but to the tribe as a whole and, by extension, to the whole Maori nation. For many Afro-Caribbean people, the extended family is much involved in tending to the needs and upbringing of the child. For aunts, uncles, older siblings to share the responsibility of the child's upbringing is a perfectly normal, reasonable, caring thing to do. Many workers in Britain, being ethnocentric in their approach – if not covertly or overtly racist – have sought to 'rescue' black children from their 'undesirable' background. in order to provide the 'best' possible chance in life – which has often been seen as placement with a white family. This would have been less problematic if those families and those professionals had been willing to address rather than deny the importance of race, culture, difference and identity. When these matters have been swept under the carpet, as was and often still is the case, clearly the child's needs have not been paramount. Contrary to the spurious melting pot theory – which might be more credible if there were more white children placed with black families – the reality is that as a result of these attitudes many black adopted people feel alienated from their roots and don't know how to regain what they have lost. They may ultimately fear rejection by the black community because they do not fit in – or do not want to 'fit in' – because they have taken on, in all but colour, a white 'identity'. Fortunately, there are many families who have recognised the different needs and priorities for the respective parties. The issues of racism, self-worth, cultural heritage and ethnic pride are treated by them, as are the individuals, with complete respect.

The most open form of adoption

What must be acknowledged is that transracial adoption is the most open adoption of all! From the child's perspective, their situation is apparent to the world. Many children are sensitive about their adoptive status. As they become more aware of, or exposed to, those situations and relationships which hinder or impair the development of self, adoption in general and transracial adoption in particular can be painful issues to confront. 'I don't want my mum to come to the school 'cause everyone asks me why I'm adopted' (12-year-old). This can threaten the sense of belonging and the need to belong. A well-meaning but ill-considered question – 'Couldn't your mother look after you, then?' – can have far-reaching, painful implications for the black child who is trying to make sense of why they are not being brought up by black people or are not more fully involved with the black community. Of course these questions, this perplexity, may not arise for some time, but the manner in which the whole issue of race and racial differences has been dealt with will have an impact on the child's ability to cope with, and to overcome, the inevitable problems they will face.

For parents – as they shop, attend Parent Teacher Association meetings, visit the hospital or surgery with their child – questions, not always articulated, may be formed in the minds of those around them: 'Where did that child come from?', 'Couldn't you have your own?' or worse: 'Couldn't you have chosen one of your *own* kind?' Such ill-considered, unkind, or downright cruel comments can chip away at the esteem of both parent and child and be one more small straw for each to carry.

Because it requires a degree of personal and interpersonal insight and understanding, an open-mindedness and a 'political' awareness which can reveal many painful realities, it is not surprising that many families have tended to deal with the issue by choosing to deny race as a factor. They consider they have friends who are emphatically not racist. Extended family members treat their adopted relatives as what indeed they are – members of the family – but implied in this is further denial of the difference both of adoption and of ethnic background, through a kind of 'benign' racism. And the Eurocentric model of the nuclear family supports and reinforces this denial of the child's right to be loved, valued and validated for themselves. This results in further denial of basic needs: esteem, belonging, understanding. How much more difficult for the child to realise their full potential if their sense of security *as a black person* is threatened – as indeed it is if the child's family does not allow the intervention or involvement (interference) of 'outsiders', alien to the nuclear family concept.

Many friends and family are not so benign, of course, nor so 'open-minded'. And it is the casual comment, the hidden barb, the simplistic yet cruel teasing which constantly reinforces the sense of difference. For many transracially adopted people, this can end up like an open wound; the feeling arises that all problems stem from the fact of adoption, and that they are made far worse because it is an ever-apparent fact.

Treating everybody the same in order to create an illusion of equality is a dangerous pretence which transracially adoptive parents are themselves beginning to challenge. There is an ever-increasing awareness and acceptance of the problems which need to be resolved, not merely for the family and their particular concerns but for our society at large. Indeed, this issue extends beyond the merely personal, even beyond the political, to the humanitarian.

Fighting the greater fight against racism
There are, sadly, many young and older transracially-adopted people who have been given *no* meaningful sense of who they are, where they come from, or where they are going. They have been patronised with the attitude that they will be treated the same as everybody else – that is, as if they were white! Many of these people, when they grow up to face the reality of racism outside the home, feel lost, angry, displaced

and disillusioned. This is not to say that their parents are bad people; they have done, as most parents do, the best they could under the circumstances. Unfortunately this best is not always enough for the black person who has to make sense of a world in which their skin colour *will* make a difference and may well be a barrier. A lack of self-esteem as a black person will be a major obstacle in many areas of endeavour.

Many white adopters are angry and hurt at the way their love and efforts seem to be discounted and devalued. It is my hope that they will use that hurt to recognise how the black community has been treated by the dominant culture in this country. It may only be through such understanding that more white parents of black youngsters become willing to fight the greater fight – not against hurtful accusations, which will pass, but against the greater evils and longer-term problems which their children will inevitably face.

The current public focus on this matter stems partly from the increased anger and frustration experienced by black adoption and social workers and other members of the ethnically visible community. Those who are concerned about the distress suffered by transracially adopted black people have felt increasingly compelled to speak out, to raise their voices against what might, at best, be described as 'benign' racism because it arose from intentions which were, generally speaking, benevolent, from motives which were good, and aspirations which were worthy.

And yet, all too often, these intentions and aspirations are deeply rooted in a white supremacist mythology based on centuries of (mis)education about the supposed inferiority of people from different cultures, races, or origins or with different physical characteristics. These attitudes have been supported by an educational and welfare system, a media, and a political structure which is invariably to the advantage of white people at the expense of black, or to the disadvantage of the poor for the benefit of the better off. The system is nurtured and the structure supported by a pattern of language which permeates every corner and level of our thinking and our doing – whether in racist humour (so-called), negative perceptions of words which mean or imply blackness, stereotypical descriptions of black people and their differences, or inherently critical denials of difference: 'I don't see you as all that black'; 'Black people are just as good as we are'.

In education, in social work, in entertainment, in literature, in legislation, in the media, and in the hearts and minds of both malicious and well-meaning people, racism is alive and well – and kicking so-called 'ethnic minorities' in the face. We must confront those who want to maintain the evil that is racism when we recognise them, but what of those who, through love, ignorance or fear, turn their eyes away from what is going on and from what they might do differently? Those who say 'We don't want to hear that, we know all about that; tell us what to do!', place the onus on black people to provide the answers – whilst blaming them for continuing to raise the issue.

For example, might not transracial adopters stop arguing with black advocates for change and lend their voices to the argument for such change? Is it not a danger sign that there is, apparently, still such a lack of understanding for the anger and suspicion expressed by so many black people about the motives and commitment of white people? Because it is not enough to pay lip-service to the notion of change: it requires action.

It is unfortunate that many white parents of black children still feel pushed into a defensive corner, as if the major issues can be resolved by convincing others that they meant well, or are doing well as adoptive parents. It is unfortunate for many reasons – a major one being that it is precisely such people who, by virtue of their position in society, their educational and social status, would be able to contribute to the battle against the deeper roots and manifestations of racism. Might not voices raised together compel local and central authorities to commit the necessary resources for minimising the harm and poison of racism?

Happily, as more and more foster carers and adoptive parents become aware of the depth and breadth of the problem, they are putting their hearts and energies into the war against this great and terrible evil which lives in closed minds in playgrounds and area offices, in court-rooms and police cells, in so many of our casual interactions with each other – in the pub, the street, the office – where young black people will not find such kindness and consideration as they are used to at home. As this awareness grows, so there is increased willingness on the part of professionals and carers to be more open in their discussions with each other and with their children.

86

Open adoption

Open adoption, I believe, is the way forward. There will be appropriate degrees of openness – some children will need protection from birth parents who constitute a real threat – but many parents, despite being, or because they are, unable to care for their children, may still wish to have some connection or involvement. As a corollary, it is clear that the majority of adopted people will, at some time in their lives, want to know about their origins, explore their roots, and may want to make some contact with birth relatives. Sadly, there are still some adopted people who are unwilling to reveal their natural, normal feelings and wishes because they fear it will hurt their adoptive parents. As the fact and theme of adoption become more open, however, and as understanding of the child's needs now or later becomes clearer, this further denial is getting rarer.

Openness may, at one extreme, be an annual telephone call from a birth parent to the social services simply asking whether the child is still alive: 'Every time I read about an accident or abduction of a child who is the same age as the child I lost to adoption, I wonder whether it was her' (birth mother). At another extreme, it may be that the birth mother takes care of her child from time to time to give the adoptive parents respite care – as happened with one severely-disabled youngster I know of. It may be letters exchanged between the families, via the social services, or regular exchanges of updates, for example for a life story book. One group of adoptive parents had the idea of sharing the cost of buying or hiring a video camera on their annual adoption day and each keeping a video of their child growing up for the birth parents, should they ever meet their child. This is evidence of a welcome generosity of spirit.

With transracial adoption, the level and nature of the contact or openness may be more complicated by the race dimension. Parents who do not understand the cultural values, the ethnic bias, the social pressures – even the national differences – which mark their child's background, may be less willing to put energy into making or maintaining contact. This may result in either the adults or the children feeling isolated with the problem and the struggle.

Perhaps local authorities could help to minimise this risk by hosting an annual adoption day for all their adopters. They could send a letter each year letting each family know that they are welcome, and people could come along to share difficulties and successes, talk things over with professionals and peers, and not feel so isolated or inadequate when things aren't going too well that they fail to ask for support until crisis has loomed and breakdown seems inevitable. Being proactive may be far more positive and constructive – and cost-effective.

Presumably much will change with the implementation of the 1989 Children Act, with its principles of partnership and paramountcy, and the definition of family (s.17[10]) as including 'any person who has parental responsibility for the child and any other person with whom [the child] has been living'. Furthermore, the child can, potentially, apply for any section 8 order including contact and residence orders. Hopefully, all this will alter the way we think about children and thus the way we approach prospective adopters. Openness should become more acceptable, and narrowness of vision more damaging, in the context not only of adoption but in our attitude towards family life in general.

Making sense of a confusion of feelings – the role of the transracially adoptive parents

Turning from the potential role of adopters in combating social racism, to their role in individual placements, it is clear that some young adopted people, despite being much loved, may still have feelings of being abandoned, depressed, guilty, grief-stricken and alienated. This is perfectly natural, although some adoptive parents' poor self-esteem cannot tolerate the expression of these feelings without their own fears of inadequacy being manifested. The feeling of being different and special (chosen), at the same time as being unloved, outcast and forsaken, contributes to a confusion familiar to adopted people of most ages. This confusion may be at its most distressing and disruptive during adolescence and, obviously, can be greatly exacerbated in a transracially adoptive family.

Ironically, when adoptive parents genuinely strive to meet the racial, cultural and ethnic needs of their children it can be extremely difficult for the youngster to talk things over without intensifying the feelings of confusion. This is often because well-meaning people unwittingly perpetuate individual, institutional and cultural strategies for shying away from the broader issues raised in challenging racism: 'I really didn't realise . . . I thought it would be enough just to take a child in . . . and to love him.' 'Well, since I understood . . . I make sure that our kids' skin and hair is properly looked after.'

Such well-meaning responses to the needs of the child are sadly inadequate. They often go hand in hand with denial of the real problems which those children are going to face, shored up by strategies like those summarised below.

Avoidance
It is accepted that 'race' is one of the dimensions in the family home but any direct confrontation is avoided. Parents adopting this strategy, when informed about racist comments or behaviour by teachers, may reply 'Well, I'm sure they didn't mean it the way you think . . . they're always OK to me' and remark to others 'Well, you've got to learn how to handle it and stand on your own two feet'.

Patronising attitudes
White 'ways' are considered superior, black ways may be tolerated. Parents in this category may, justifiably, object to the clamour of their child's friends but fail to acknowledge the child's interpretation of these objections. 'Ethnic' food, clothing, arts and crafts may be brought out 'on special occasions'; magazines and newspapers may be brought into the house but never seriously read by anybody but black family members. A subtle 'them' and 'us' message pervades.

Omission
Parents, friends, educators, doctors and others may refuse to accept the racial dimension of interaction between the child and themselves. They prefer to argue either that 'things aren't that bad . . . they are getting better', or even that racism doesn't exist at all – especially in their own homes and hearts. The kindly family friend or neighbour who makes racist comments and then accuses the child of having a chip on their shoulder if they react falls into this grouping.

Denial
This is refusal to accept that racism is anything more than the extreme personal prejudices of irrational people. It encompasses the denial of the cultural and institutional forms of racism apparent everywhere. The youth training officer who said that he didn't see colour when people came through the door, then added that the young black people who attended his scheme were lazy and

unmotivated, that there was plenty of work available but they didn't seem to want it, provides a good example of this stance.

Colour blindness
This is a particularly prevalent attitude in transracially adoptive families: 'I treat all my children the same!' – and one of the many ways in which black people's specific experience and expectation of life in Britain can be negated.

Dumping
This process is one in which the black people are blamed for the problem on the one hand – 'Don't you think you'd get on better if you didn't make such a fuss?', 'No wonder people get upset when black people are so aggressive!', 'Well, why aren't there more black families available to look after black kids?' – and, on the other hand, are expected to find their own solution without the input of necessary resources or support.

If, as parents or as adoption workers, these levels of awareness can be expanded – if the good intentions can be turned into action which confronts the broader issues of personal, cultural and institutional racism – the world into which our children grow may become a little less fraught, a little more loving. Openness in all areas of adoption can help promote movement towards that change.

The experience of young transracially adopted people
It is not enough, indeed it is arrogance on any parent's part, to believe that the love they offer will suffice for life beyond the family home. Yet, in working through the tasks of adolescence, biological children have a sense of continuity, a link with past generations, a family identity which the adopted child simply does not have. This, like so many other aspects of adoption, is compounded when the adoption is transracial because the child has to make sense of their place in a world where, every day, the differences are manifest, where frequently they will have to struggle with the fact of racism, yet may feel isolated in a family which does not share that experience. A heartfelt cry from a transracially adopted 16-year-old – 'If I accept that same-race placements are the right ones then I have to say that my childhood is wiped away' – indicates only too clearly that isolation,

where the need for understanding has not been met. Security is threatened, in the sense of the child wondering where they fit into the overall picture of society as well as finding a place in the family.

Children often fantasise that their parents are not really their parents. For adopted people this has an added poignancy because there is an element of truth in it. Where their adoption is evident to all and, they may imagine, their feelings apparent, there is still one more burden for the child to carry. If this and associated issues are not resolved, the child may attribute good and bad qualities to the adoptive and biological families separately. This may then be magnified across whole cultures so that they come to believe that black equals negative and white equals positive and this, in turn, may be reinforced in the adoptive family by the avoidance strategies mentioned above. Or the opposite may occur and the children come to believe that all white people are bad, or untrustworthy, or unsafe, so that they cannot discuss racism with their parents because they know they will not understand and cannot empathise, and the white social worker is no better.

Adolescents need to test out the security of home and their place in the hierarchy. This they may do by acting out, arguing, perhaps rejecting everything the parents stand for. Again, this is perfectly natural as part of the development of self and of identity. What then are youngsters to do if they have little or no information – or only negative information – about black people, black families, black culture? They may come to believe that they themselves are bad and may try on other personas which fit the stereotypes.

If adoptive parents have not resolved their own doubts and anxieties – have not, for example, come fully to terms with their own sense of loss or the inadequacy which many feel about infertility – they may have problems understanding or accepting their child's burgeoning sexuality. This is another problem they share with the vast majority of parents but which has additional connotations in a society which holds strong stereotypes about the sexuality of young black men and women. Or, if the parents have not acknowledged and confronted their own racism, they may well try to suppress the child's challenging rather than seeing it as the natural process of exploring individuality. It is virtually impossible for a white person to understand the black experience, although it *is* possible for people to discount that experience by making false comparisons: 'It was exactly the same for me, coming down to London from Yorkshire'; 'I know how you feel, darling, I didn't like my teachers either'; 'I *could* understand, if only you'd tell me what's wrong!' The young adopted person may well, then, need other supports outside the immediate adoptive family to accomplish the tasks of growing up and of developing a confident black identity.

It is also during adolescence that the adopted person really begins to understand what adoption means in terms of personal loss: they have lost a biological and cultural link, a portion of their personal narrative – something crucial is missing. It is not as simple as knowing about adoption, nor is it to do with having information or a life story book with pictures – although that would help, as would offering all parties the opportunity to exchange annual update letters and using the area office as a poste-restante to show respect for the child's eventual need to know, or the adult's eventual need for contact. For transracially adopted adolescents this loss is felt with increased intensity, and may lead to questions about their status, their value, their parents – both biological and adoptive. The strength of these emotions may make it difficult for the youngster to express them to parents they love and do not want to hurt, or with whom they feel unable to discuss or share their pain. And how often, sadly, does the pain explode as aggression or teenage rebellion? If adopted people have detected a reluctance or experienced a silence around the issues of origins, birth parents, racial differences, even adoption itself, this may make it still more difficult to open the subject, let alone to explore what it means, explain how it feels or know what to do about it. If their parents have no black friends, or only those who aspire to white middle-class values and do not accept the feelings which the transracially-placed child may experience, this may be another area of potential conflict. A general openness can preclude many of these problems, and open adoption may eradicate them entirely.

Physical changes, awareness of themselves as sexual beings who could procreate, may produce a new sense of bewilderment, even abandonment now they too can become a parent: 'Would I do what my parents did?'; 'Is there something genetically wrong with me?'; 'Can I make up for my own abandonment?'; 'Would my own child love me?' Again, without claiming it to be a universal panacea, openness in adoption may be the difference that makes the difference!

Sexuality is one of the major concerns of adolescence and this will undoubtedly be affected by the attitude of the family. This attitude will be at least influenced, and probably largely determined, by cultural and social 'norms' – which, by definition, often exclude or denounce those who are different. As was mentioned earlier, there are many myths about black people's sexuality and sexual behaviour: 'They breed like rabbits'; 'They have loads of kids, then leave them to be looked after by others'; 'They're all promiscuous'. If the white parents of black children have not dealt with their own prejudices on this score, they may either confirm by silence or, by casual comments, add to the child's confusion about their sexual identity. This is another area where openness can make a profound difference for everybody concerned – although it is perhaps the most difficult because of the still prevalent taboos about sexuality.

If infertility was a motivation for adoption and the parents have not resolved their own grief, which is frequently the case even after many years, or if they do not realise that it is an undercurrent in their dealings with fertile youngsters, the normal conflicts between parents and teenagers, already complicated by the adoptive status, may become raging torrents of emotion which are almost impossible for anybody to cope with.

Some families come to the Post-Adoption Centre because the emotions have exploded so often, the pressure has been so great, the pain so severe, that they arrive wondering if they are beyond hope and help. They may well have been to one professional after another – psychologists, educational welfare offices, family therapists – to little or no avail. The child may have been pathologised, described as schizophrenic, seen as so different as to be beyond redemption. This may be interpreted as 'bad blood' and the birth parents 'blamed', sometimes directly and in so many words, for the child's behaviour. But, again, these patterns are not unusual or abnormal. The particular dimension of adoption adds new elements to sexuality issues, and transracial adoption is an area of greater danger, greater stress, greater bias. Openness can help reduce some of this tension.

Some ways forward

This chapter has been based on personal experience and on contact with many people from different corners of the adoption triangle: white adoptive parents, black teenagers, children and adults who were adopted by white parents, black birth parents, as well as black and white professionals, and people who have been involved in some aspect of open adoption. All the quotations are genuine, and all were made recently.

For those parents and professionals who are involved with young children who are being, or have been, transracially placed (whether through adoption or fostering), for professionals who supervise or teach other professionals, there are certain things you can consider which may alert you to some of the danger areas. This certainly does not mean that the problem will go away, and it does not mean that you will have done all that you could, if you were to address these specific areas. But it does mean that you may create a climate in which those youngsters, those adults in the making, may feel more supported, better understood, more validated and valued for their uniqueness and strengths, whilst the very real difficulties they will have to face in a racist society are acknowledged.

Some questions to ask yourself:

- Have I proactively sought out more information in an attempt to increase my understanding and awareness of racism? What resources, books, conversations, arguments have I come across or been involved in lately?

- To what extent do I explore whether my own (un)conscious attitudes are actively contributing to or combating racism?

- Do I investigate the stance and activities of political candidates?

- Have I done anything to promote or contribute to raising awareness with friends, colleagues, church groups, clubs, schools?

- Have I openly disagreed with racist comments, jokes or actions when I witness them?

- To what extent am I aware of racism in the media, and how do I deal with it?

- Do I constantly re-evaluate my own attitudes and behaviour to check whether they might be perceived as racist, degrading or hurtful?

5 The spread of openness in New Zealand – the two ends of the process meeting in the middle

Audrey Mullender

The concept of openness can be present or absent at all stages of the adoption process. We might think of it, however, as currently having two major manifestations in British practice: the making of a proportion of new adoption placements which involve direct contact, and opening up situations which were previously closed through access to birth records after the adopted person has reached adulthood.

Opening up closed placements before adulthood

In New Zealand, these two areas – the making of placements and the issue of adults having access to recorded information – are handled as very separate matters. They are covered by different legislation, which is the responsibility of different Government departments, and they are normally dealt with by different teams of staff within the Department of Social Welfare (DSW). Even so, increasingly, these two ends of the process of opening up placements are meeting in the middle, often because the members of the adoption triad themselves wish it – that is, because adopted people below the age of majority (20 in New Zealand) are increasingly asking that their placements should be opened up, or because their adoptive parents are asking them if they would like to do this, or because their birth parents are reaching a stage where they wish that they had kept in touch and seek to re-open contact.

The parties have no legal rights to try and turn a completely closed placement into an open one before the adopted person is 20 unless both the birth parent(s) and the adoptive family have separately made contact with the agency to request this. If there is a one-sided request for contact or information in a closed adoption, only non-identifying information can be provided by the post-adoption worker. (Non-identifying information is specifically not affected by the Adult Adoption Information Act and, hence, can be freely communicated.) Non-identifying information passed on to a birth parent would

95

normally consist only of material recorded on the file in the period up to the making of the final order, unless the adoptive family has been in touch with the department since then. It would include facts about the adopters (but not names): ages, jobs (unless so unusual as to be likely to lead to identification, especially as occupations appear on the electoral register in New Zealand), and home environment; the child's adoptive first name (again, unless it is too unusual) and any details which were recorded about the baby, although the file often just says 'good progress'. Another possibility is to run a family benefit check on the family which shows whether they are still living in New Zealand, and whether the child is still at school or has left in the past year. This is a way of providing a useful up-date without contacting the family.

Many birth parents are pleased to have even this information because they have often believed they were not entitled to anything at all. The publicity given to the change in the law making identifying information available stressed that it would only apply in cases where the adopted person was aged at least 20, so many birth parents never consider contacting the DSW before that. Yet the non-identifying information which can be released may at least take away the desperation of knowing nothing.

At the same time as communicating the above non-identifying facts to a birth parent, one post-adoption worker I spoke to sends them a questionnaire requesting all the information she needs to up-date her file. Then, if approached by the adopted person later on, she will have it ready. The sorts of thing she asks is whether the birth parent is married or single, whether they have experienced any health problems since the child was placed, and whether they would want to be contacted by the adopted person if the latter should get in touch with the department. Many birth parents are very pleased that this is noted on the file, although it can never satisy those who are desperate for contact straight away.

The only exception to the limitations on the one-sided situation just described is if the birth parent is, for example, dying of cancer, or has discovered that he or she has a hereditary illness and a doctor says in writing that it is essential to contact the adoptive family. Similarly, the Adult Adoption Information Act provides for essential medical and genetic counselling information to be traced by means of birth records, at the request of a doctor, but without identifying information being revealed. Some campaigners in New Zealand see this as a breach in the wall of secrecy and feel that this should now be widened to allow contact following all one-sided approaches, even where the adopted person has not yet reached the age of 20.

Some workers responsible for post-placement work are already willing to go further than the norm and to bend the rules somewhat. If they receive a one-sided request for contact, they will scour the file for some sign of earlier interest from the other party, such as a birth mother who kept in contact for a year after the birth to find out about the baby's progress, or adopters who requested photographs of the birth mother, and will then approach them to see if contact would be welcomed. At least one team of workers also has a policy of encouraging people, if they have a sufficiently strong 'special ground', to apply for closed records to be opened through the courts, as part of a broader move to convince the judiciary of the need to end secrecy overall.

Opening up semi-open placements

There is no hindrance whatsoever to any of the parties seeking to make a somewhat open placement completely open, and many do so. In the early years, contact may be maintained through the post-adoption worker. Typically, the birth parent and adopters meet once in the very earliest stages and know each other only on first name terms. Before the order is made, often when the child is aged about ten months, the adopters tend to write their own reports on the progress of the child and their feelings about the placement and these, together with photos, the birth parents receive. Subsequently, letters and photos will tend to be sent periodically, at least at significant times such as the child starting school, using the Department of Social Welfare as a postbox. Christmas is always a very busy time, for example. This opportunity to exchange information and to acknowledge special times is positive for everyone.

When it comes to seem inadequate, however, a not untypical pattern is for the situation to move up a gear about five to 10 years after placement – when the adopters feel ready for it to do so. By this time, the family unit is well established and the adopters feels secure in their entitlement to the child and in their ability to be good parents. A few bump into the birth parent by accident and pick up from there; a not inconsiderable number tell the post-adoption worker (or social worker in a denominational agency) that they now feel confident enough to open up the placement.

One example concerns a family who had adopted eight years before. There had been annual correspondence ever since and the adopters got to the point of feeling 'Oh, blow this, why don't we just meet?' They did so and all the parties felt very positive about it. In another case, a social worker I talked to had helped to renegotiate an arrangement on behalf of a birth mother who was in letter contact but who now regretted never having met the adopters. The adoption worker rang them and was well received on the phone so had a lengthy meeting with them before they met the birth mother. After that, the placement became a fully open one.

This does not mean that everything necessarily proceeds smoothly or easily all the time. Adoptive families may face changes in their, the child's or the birth parent's situation, or times when their relationship with the child or birth parents hits problems. The post-adoption social worker has a role in responding to requests to discuss the best course of action at such times. While I was in New Zealand, for example, a Catholic Social Services social worker was just helping to set up a group for adoptive families to meet one another and talk over just such difficulties, at the behest of an adoptive parent of two children.

The advantages of increased openness
Social workers involved in post-adoption work in New Zealand are strongly of the view that exchange of information, preferably including actual contact, is positive for everyone involved.

For the child, information received direct from his or her birth parent answers all sorts of questions with reality rather than incomplete 'don't know's, guesses or fantasy, and it gives the child someone who, from photos at least, they can see they look like. Where they begin to meet their birth parents, this does not have the same feel as access visits to children in care. Rather than being heavily structured, it quickly becomes spontaneous with people dropping in when they are in that part of the country or arranging shared activities.

For the adopters, direct information is provided for passing on to their child rather than struggling with questions they cannot answer. Having actually met the birth parent(s) early on, they are more able to convey a positive and warm picture of them as people and less able to forget that the child has another family and is entitled to know about them. With up-to-date information continuing to arrive, they are helped to discuss the child's adopted status and background freely. This is very much to be welcomed but still does not always happen in Britain. It also means that adoptive parents can share their joy in their growing child with someone they know also cares very much about him or her. In fact, adopters are often the keenest party to maintain contact once it has begun, simply because they enjoy sharing news of their child.

For the birth parent(s), information is crucial, especially early on, saving all the pain of not knowing how the child is (or even whether he or she is still alive), knowing something about who the adopters are, and being given up-to-date news about the child's progress. Having been involved in choosing these adopters and in meeting them, the birth-parent(s) can feel a part of the process and that they have done the best for their child. It also means they can acknowledge birthdays and Christmas, which tend to be times when they are very much thinking of the child in any case. Because they have this information, birth parents do not have the desperate need to know that we are still hearing about it in Britain. They feel comfortable in the knowledge that they can ring up the post-adoption social worker at any time for an up-date. They are not stuck in the past like birth parents who have experienced only the secrecy model, but are freer to get on with their own lives. In doing so, they may drop out of contact with the DSW for a while and the adopters can then feel quite disappointed. One Auckland social worker told me she had recently had adopters on the phone in tears because their child's birth mother was getting married and had said she wanted no further contact. Iwanek[1] notes that birth parents may reach a point of wanting only minimal contact precisely when the adopters feel comfortable enough to want more. This could be raised by the social worker at the time of placement as something to prepare for, as well as reminding the participants that the arrangements belong to the parties and can be renegotiated at any time, although the social worker is available to give assistance if required.

One social worker I spoke to wondered whether some young adopted people, as the years go by, may not be all that interested in the set-up their adoptive and birth parents have negotiated and may wonder what all the fuss is about. I certainly met one young man who expressed those views but he does phone and sometimes meet his birth mother of his own accord so obviously does not feel negative about it. It is not damaging for the child to have contact they feel somewhat indifferent about, but it is damaging to lack contact when you want it. Most often the birth parent becomes another special person in the life of the adopted child, who does not appear to experience confusion about these different sets of parents. These children say quite clearly that they know who Mum and Dad are – those who have brought them up – but that it is good to have another Mother and sometimes another Father. The evidence is that where adopters have had an earlier, closed adoption and a later, open one, they greatly prefer, and feel more comfortable with, the open one and it provides a spur to open up the earlier placement. Sometimes, then, adoptive parents are pushing social workers along, which belies the stereotypes one still comes across in Britain – that adopters would not be able to deal with openness.

The minority who fear openness – the role of law and practice

There are still a minority of adopters who harbour fears of losing their child through openness and who agree to ongoing letters and photos only in order to get the baby, intending to cut off contact once the order is made. The situation in New Zealand is that contact cannot be made a condition of the order, as it can in Britain – and the birth parent has no redress if the adopters renege on their promises. Most practitioners believe that legal constraint would not work and that only goodwill, trust and negotiation are effective. Iwanek, on the other hand, argues that, just as adopters feel more secure when they get the legal protection of the adoption order, so birth parents should enjoy the same kind of protection and legal recognition of their more limited rights. She sees relationships as more likely to work when parties are legally regarded as equals, rather than the birth parents being in an unequal and powerless position as now. Legislating for open adoption will, she believes, 'enhance responsible decision making as it will encourage all parties to consider their decisions more carefully and thus exclude those applicants who enter an initial agreement with the intention of stopping contact after an adoption order is made, which has been the experience of a number of birth parents.'[2] Also, she feels, it would protect the interests of the child

100

through guaranteeing access to both families. There has been a suggestion in a review of New Zealand's 1955 Adoption Act (still the relevant legislation) of introducing contracts to be tied in with the consent, setting out agreed conditions of placements based on the wishes of both birth and adoptive parents, but falling short of threatening the placement if not carried out. This has never been acted on, however.

In a very few cases, post-adoption workers in New Zealand have come across adopters like those mentioned above who appear to have agreed to everything they were asked to do but without the intention of carrying it out. Even under circumstances where adopters have gone back on their promises, it is usually possible to invite them into the office and to talk to them about what their real fears are – of losing their child, of course. These are usually resolvable, with work and reassurance. All that may be needed in such cases is for the adopters to discuss with a post-placement worker why contact is helpful for the child, how others have experienced it and what is right for them as a family, leading sometimes to renegotiation with the birth parent(s) so that the adopters feel more in control. They have to find an arrangement which works for them.

Although later support is crucial, it seems quite probable that adopters feel able to go as far as the model held by the agency and the worker(s) who prepare them for their placement leads them. Those who adopt through Catholic Social Services in Christchurch, for example, feel comfortable with complete openness from the start,[3] whereas Department of Social Welfare adopters in some areas prefer a semi-confidential model to start with but not infrequently open it up later on. It is probably the agency's courage which varies, rather than that of the adopters, since the latter may outstrip the former as time goes on. Preparation of prospective adopters is crucial, both in communicating the agency's ideas on openness and in freeing up adopters to take these on board.

One key factor seems to be the extent to which birth parents are involved in preparation programmes. If adopters have had ample opportunity to meet face to face and to explode their myths about birth parents – who they are and what they want – these myths are less likely to hang around and interfere with what is possible later on. Many adopters have said that the biggest single influence in convincing them about open adoption was meeting and talking to

101

birth parents during their preparation evenings or weekends. It then becomes impossible, for example, to think of all birth mothers as irresponsible young girls who got drunk and became pregnant by someone they did not know and who, if it were not for adopters, would be forced to scrounge off the State, or as desperately unhappy women who want to grab their babies back at the first opportunity. Meeting birth mothers and hearing their story helps adopters to think of them, instead, as real people who love and care about their children and who also have feelings and needs of their own.

The importance of birth parents in the openness debate

The trend towards greater openness has enormous implications, then, for all members of the adoption triad but it perhaps hinges most crucially on changing attitudes towards birth parents. These changes have been slower to register in Britain but are at last beginning to make an impact. There are now at least two organisations for birth parents in this country; one, the Birth Mothers' Support Group, sprang from a group run at the Post-Adoption Centre, and the other, the Natural Parents' Support Group, featured on Open Space on BBC2 in March 1988. This is, as yet, a very young and small campaign compared to the situation both in Australia and in New Zealand.

The long established history, high profile, and keen campaigning stance of equivalent groups in New Zealand can be taken as one measure of the difference. One of the most vocal groups is the Aotearoa Birthmothers' Support Group in Auckland. It is for women who have lost a child by adoption. Actually now a collective of four support groups, it started in 1985 'out of a common need for women to support women thinking about, starting to search and on making contact with their daughter or son' (ABSG information leaflet, undated). The group's publicity leaflet tells pregnant women their rights, including that they need not feel pressurised into making a decision, sets out the group's campaigning platform (arguing, for example, that guardianship should completely replace adoption), explodes myths about birth mothers, and discusses the severe effects of relinquishment as a different kind of grief which, it is claimed, increases rather than reduces over time. The leaflet sums up the group's position as follows:

The secrecy needed by society to cope with adoption imposes guilt, shame, worthlessness and loss of self esteem on women, ultimately

102

affecting their emotional, psychological, physical and spiritual health.

In New Zealand, an important catalyst in the development of this movement away from secrecy and towards openness in adoption was the publication of a hard-hitting book, written by a birth mother, called *Death by adoption*.[4] (See also Inglis,[5] on relinquishing mothers in Australia, and Howarth[6] writing in New Zealand from accounts by adopted people.) Billed on the flyleaf as a 'radical feminist book', it is dedicated to 'childless mothers everywhere who put society's decision into action by signing adoption consent'. The cruel treatment of birth parents in the not-so-distant past is, indeed, very much a feminist issue, not only because of the way birth mothers were treated as 'fallen women'; but also, I would argue, in the way birth fathers have been largely ignored. Pregnancy was seen as the birth mother's guilty responsibility and she was left literally 'holding the baby'.

Open adoption confronts these issues of sexual mores and goes a long way towards rehabilitating the birth parents, both by involving them in their children's lives on a continuing basis and by giving them real choices. What prevented openness in the past was the harsh and punititve attitude of society towards birth mothers. They were denied access to their adopted children while those children were growing up and also later, when they reached adulthood. At the same time, they were unable to be a reality to their children who had to make do with sketchy information and a shadowy presence in the background. Both birth parents and adopted people have thus been losers. The challenge to adopters and to social workers is to prevent this from happening in the future. Opening up placements that were previously closed is one way of rehabilitating birth parents: of acknowledging both that they have rights and that they have much to offer to the children they bore but can no longer care for.

Have the two ends met in the middle in Britain?
Here in the UK, since the belated implementation of the requirement of the 1976 Adoption Act that a unified adoption service should be provided by every adoption agency, we ought more easily to be able to conceptualise all the aspects of adoption as inter-related. Yet the lessons so painfully learnt from birth records counselling – that adopted people do need to know as much as possible about who they are and who their families are – and from listening to the anguish of

103

birth parents, do not always seem to have filtered down to those working at the other end of the process – the making of placements.

In baby placements, it does seem to be becoming more common for birth parents and adopters to meet but is this yet uniform procedure and are birth parents yet fully involved in the choice of adoptive parents for their child? In New Zealand, although only a small proportion of Department of Social Welfare placements are made as completely open placements with continuing meetings between the parties, no placement seems to fall below the degree of openness represented by one meeting and letter contact thereafter. Do any do so here? And, even though the secrecy model has been well and truly breached in this country, do we still have too powerful an 'expertise' model for social work practice? In a radio programme broadcast during 1990, for example, a 'typical' placement was followed through all its stages. The birth mother spelled out her requirements in the adopters, and the social workers chose the couple following what she had said as far as possible, although there had to be some compromises and it was the social workers who decided what these should be. The birth mother and adopters met once after the birth and the birth mother talked about the pain of knowing they would not meet again, though she hoped her child would come looking for her at the age of 18. Although she knew she could get news of him through the adoption agency should she want it, neither she nor the adopters were in charge of the situation. Rather, it rested in official hands to judge what was best for all concerned.

Especially worryingly, in relation to placements from care, one still too ofter hears about termination of parental access before adoption, as if permanence and being cut off from one's roots were the same thing. This is an area of practice in which we cannot learn lessons from New Zealand because they have not used adoption as a solution to that kind of situation. We have to develop our own solutions, and perhaps one of these could be a less ready use of heavily interventionary models in child care practice. New Zealand social workers find our heavy use of place of safety orders, termination of access, and contested adoptions very odd. It goes against their increasing stress, reinforced by new child care legislation, on involving families routinely in decision-making processes. Even in the most severe cases, parents are fully involved. One permanency worker argued to me that if she were to use a model of adoption based on dispensing with consent, the birth parent might terminate contact – and she saw this as too great a risk to run. How odd this sounds in our context, and yet how much healthier for all concerned.

Conclusions – implications for social workers

The challenge to social workers in Britain, then, is to carry to their logical conclusion the changing attitudes towards birth parents – to give them rights, not to pathologise them, and to involve them far more in new and existing adoptive placements.

Why do social workers in Britain set up therapeutic groups rather than campaigning groups for birth mothers? Our attitude towards them should be to see them not as bad or sick, but as women who carry the legacy of a hyprocritical and victim-blaming society. Birth parents' own self-help groups are beginning to speak out now, and to demand that further generations of women do not have to face what they went through. The Birth Mothers' Support Group has drawn attention to women who, even now, are placing babies without real choices and/or without the support they need to understand the momentous consequences of a closed adoption. Professionals and consumers together need to take this on as an issue. Similarly, current practice with families who lose older children to adoption must learn to look for the strengths in birth parents or other relatives and to assess whether they do still have something to offer to the child, perhaps under circumstances of greater professional surveillance and support than would be the case following a baby placement.

Whatever developments the future may hold, the overwhelming challenge to professionals in both New Zealand and Britain is to recognise, as John Triseliotis has put it, that 'adoption work is by its nature seductive because of the amount of power it transfers to its practitioners'.[7] In fact, it is already possible to see the enormous distance that practice has travelled from the time when it was possible for Martin Davies to write:

> The social worker has almost absolute power to facilitate or prevent the process of adoption. He [sic] selects adoptive parents, advises the natural mother, and allocates the child.[8]

In New Zealand, all three parts of this statement are now inaccurate. Adopters are involved in deciding whether adoption is right for them. Work with the birth mother bears less resemblance to 'advice' and more to facilitating her in making her own choice – a choice that she can live with for the rest of her life. And it is now the birth mother or birth parents together who decide who should adopt their child. Social workers have an important new style of role to play in assisting this process at all its stages, and in preparing adopters and birth parents to meet one another and to make the most of the contact that follows.

It is time to admit that we cannot judge who will make the best parents or which marriages or placements will last, because no measures exist on which to base such claims. Rather, adopters are the experts on what they can offer a child and birth parents on what they want for their child. We need a revolution in attitudes to birth parents away from what Ann Corcoran has called 'the "there there dear we know best" syndrome' (unpublished conference paper) to treating them as responsible adults.

We also need a whole new philosophy of social work practice which is consumer-led, rather than pseudo-expert-led. Social workers will continue to require a high level of skills and knowledge but these will need to be harnessed in different ways in future. To quote Iwanek again: 'The role of the social worker in open adoption is therefore one of educating, supporting, facilitating, enabling and empowering people to make their own decisions, believing in the notion that people know what is best for them in most situations.' This will include knowing when increased openness is desirable and what level of support is needed in placements which were previously closed.

References

1 Iwanek M (1987) 'A study of open adoption placements: the experiences over a period of time of 17 adoptive families and 14 birth mothers who had entered into an open adoption arrangement' Lower Hutt, New Zealand: Department of Social Welfare (unpublished), 1987.

2 See 1 above.

3 Howell D and Ryburn M 'New Zealand: new ways to choose adopters', *Adoption & Fostering*, 11 4, 1987.

4 Shawyer J *Death by adoption*, Auckland, New Zealand: Cicada Press, 1979.

5 Inglis K *Living mistakes: mothers who consented to adoption* Sydney: George Allen and Unwin, 1984.

6   Howarth A *Reunion: adoption and the search for birth origins – the New Zealand story,* Auckland: Penguin, 1988.

7   Triseliotis J 'Some moral and practical issues in adoption work' *Adoption & Fostering* 13 2, 1989.

8   Davies M *The essential social worker: a guide to positive practice* London: Heinemann, 1981.

THE PERSPECTIVE OF BIRTH MOTHERS

6 Closed adoption – a lifetime loss

Doreen Ward

I can remember that as soon as I knew about sex and sexuality, I also knew that if I became pregnant before I was married, it would be the worst thing that could happen to me and my family. As teenagers, friends and I would talk about the fears of being sent to homes for unmarried mothers, which held the same horrors for us as prisons might have done – in fact we believed that they were probably worse than prison.

When I suspected that I was pregnant, at the age of 19, I felt that my life had come to an end. I could see no way through or out of the nightmare. I was training to be a nurse and when the matron knew of the pregnancy she asked me to leave and not to return as I would set a bad example to other nurses. I knew that it would be impossible to live at home, seeing the distress that I was causing my parents, so I chose the only alternative – a home for unmarried mothers. I was seen by a moral welfare worker who suggested a home in a northern city where I could go almost immediately, so at three months pregnant I moved into a house with 10 or so other 'girls' and waited for the nightmare to end.

We were all going to have our babies adopted. This was such a foregone conclusion that it hardly merited any discussion amongst us. The babies were born at the 'home' and we were obliged to look after them for six weeks after the birth, including breast-feeding for the first month. This was the only aspect of the proceedings that we discussed, as we waited for our time to come. We wondered if it would be better if the babies were taken away as soon as they were born, and believed that the reason we had to look after them for six weeks was to punish us even more for being pregnant and unmarried. We also noticed that some women changed their minds during that time and did not proceed with the adoption, but all of us were resolute that we were not going to do that.

During all those months before the birth there was no ante-natal care, apart from very basic physical check-ups, and absolutely no

111

counselling from anybody about the major decision we had made about the lives of these babies yet to be born. We understood without it needing to be said that all babies deserved two parents, one male and one female, who were married to each other and had sufficient financial security to care for our babies in the ways that we could not. We saw these unknown couples as much better people than we were.

My daughter was born in the late summer after a long and terrifying labour and, true to the ethos of the place, nobody said 'congratulations'. We did all the physical caring for our babies but were only allowed into the nursery at feed-times, although we could take the babies out for two hours in the afternoons. We used to go to a little park round the corner from the home and talk about superficial things as we pushed the prams. Nobody dared to say anything upsetting, and there was nobody to help us. I think we all closed our minds to what we were doing – apart from those, of course, who had 'changed their minds'. By the time I left, half those resolute women had decided to keep their babies, and I was completely lost as to how that change had come about. Looking back, I now see that they were the ones whose families, or friends, or lovers, visited them and showed that they would support them should they choose to keep the baby. I was angry with them for breaking the code. Maybe I was deeply envious that they could.

A month after my daughter was born, I was interviewed by the adoption officer who asked me a few basic questions about health and family. There were no questions about how I felt. I was told a few days later that a family had been found and I would be leaving the day before my daughter was six weeks old. We were together for 41 days.

I was given no choice about the type of family I would like for my daughter, very little information about them, and was never offered an opportunity to talk about this momentous time in our lives. I already felt that she was their daughter, not mine, and that I was looking after her on their behalf. I never met them, only heard their voices in the next room as she was taken from me and through to them. I shut my mind to them and her and went to find my life again, where I had left it some months before.

But, of course, it wasn't the same. I had changed, my body had changed, and the denial of that was a little like madness, but the finality of it all, the complete ending of my brief motherhood, meant that it was impossible for me to stay connected to the fact that I had once had a baby. I was supposed to care about her so much that I would give her to a good home and proper family, yet that caring was then supposed to cease abruptly as she was carried from one room to another, and after that I felt that I was just not allowed to care any more. It seemed that this was forbidden because it was too great a threat to her new family.

Closed adoption of this sort is like a bereavement without a death, and lacking the accompanying rituals that are appropriate to death. There is a void into which fantasies and pain are put; pain that cannot be resolved because somewhere, there is somebody living and growing in other people's lives, though not in yours. I could never talk about my first child to anybody because I thought that I would be judged harshly for having given away my own baby, and my feelings of self-worth were so low that I would have felt that judgement to be correct. The complete severance of all ties with her has been a continual reinforcement of that negative view of myself – the view that started in pregnancy and which has shown itself in different ways over the subsequent years.

When I told my second daughter about her elder sister she was fascinated and distressed. She had acquired a sister but lost her again, and this sense of loss is compounded by the total lack of knowledge about her and her current life. But for me, being able to tell my second daughter and my son about their elder sister was the start of my being able to acknowledge her existence to myself.

How different this would have been if I had continued to have news of my daughter's welfare and life – I could have put reality in the place of fantasy. It has been almost impossible to imagine my daughter as a growing child, and now an adult woman, not a six-week old baby frozen in time and existing in a black-and-white photograph. To many birth mothers, one piece of information or one photograph of their child's new life would have felt like a very open adoption compared to complete silence. We would have felt recognised and valued as somebody significant in our children's lives, even though we could not contine to be the nurturers of those lives.

As I have been helped to understand the lifetime implications, for me, of having lost my first child in this way, I have allowed my daughter to grow up in my mind. I have also become more compassionate to the 19-year-old who made that decision to have her child adopted all those years ago. I feel that I, too, have grown up.

7 Open adoption – a birth mother's personal view

Penelope

I would like to contrast my experience of a closed adoption with the more open adoption which I believe would have been possible and preferable for me and my son.

When my son was adopted as a baby in 1973, the people involved could not predict his future. We made decisions which were based on our hopes and visions of his future life. The adoption society hoped that they had found a suitable man and woman to become his parents. The couple, who were childless, had their own hopes for bringing up a child and tried to imagine what this would be like. I hoped he would grow up knowing he was adopted, and with the encouragement and love of his new family.

I have always recognised the reality of my son growing up with a new name in a permanent family who are strangers to me. I imagine him doing the same things as other children his age. His birthdays have been important steps in his development as well as reminders of his birth. My starting points are the first month of his life while I cared for him in hospital, the afternoon we had alone together, letters from the adoption society describing his life in his new home, and a photograph. Since the adoption I have had no information. The difficulty I face is that I have only imagination and fantasy to enable me to accept and live with the reality of my son's adoption and growing up. When he was 15 I had a vivid dream of meeting and saying goodbye to him which brought together all I knew and imagined.

I also feel uncomfortable knowing that to my son and his adoptive parents I too am a fantasy, frozen in a time capsule for 16 years. My son only knows what his parents have told him. They only know what the adoption worker chose to tell them from the answers I gave to her questions.

The lack of information has affected me and my family in several ways. The first is the lack of anything new to say which would be the natural way to talk about any member of my family. I find it impossible to talk about my son to relatives who are younger than he is. If I did, he would still seem unreal to them. If a more open adoption had been available, the following is what I would like to have been able to tell my family and friends.

My son lives with one of the couples recommended to me by the adoption agency. After I met them they fostered him while arrangements for the adoption and continuing contact were agreed. We now meet about every six months, around the times of his birthday and mine. My son has met my parents, and sisters and brother. He shares some interests with them. This may be genetic, but is more likely to be because I chose as adopters the couple who would give him some of the opportunities and values which are important in my own family. When he is 18, my son will be as clear about his origins and identity as any other young man.

For me, this very natural and realistic story is a fantasy, but I believe it should be a reality for others.

I have recently written to a social worker who has access to some reports on my son and his family. I have received in return a short letter telling me very little. Reading this letter made me realise that I could not even assume that he had survived infancy. Even that had to be imagined. Yet in the news media, there are so many reminders of the vulnerability of children.

I now have a clear view of myself as separated by adoption from a young adult who will soon have a choice whether and when to find out more about me. I hope that this personal view will explain why I have never felt that I should try to forget my son. It also shows why I resent being told that by continuing to think about him I am 'living in the past'.

8 On behalf of birth parents
Phillida Sawbridge

'If I could only know if she is alive or dead.'

These words, or something very like them, have probably been spoken by at least 1,500 of the more than 1,600, almost all white, birth mothers of adopted children who contacted the Post-Adoption Centre in its first four years of existence. Most of them would probably laugh rather hollowly if asked what they thought about open adoption. The experience of most women who parted with a child 15, 20 or 30 years ago was that there was not even a hair-line crack in the wall of silence, let alone a suggestion of openness.

It is new for the views of birth parents to be considered at all in a context such as this. Legislation directly affecting them has been passed without access to their views. Very little adoption literature refers to them more than in passing, and 1988 was probably the first year in which anyone prepared to be labelled as a 'birth mother' actually spoke publicly at a social work conference in England.

The views of those who lost the most
It is quite a staggering thought that, although adoption has existed in England and Wales since 1926, the views of the people who suffered most by it and lost most through it, have been totally unknown to the social workers who have continued making adoption placements for over 60 years.

I have been one of those social workers; I too have placed children with little thought for how the birth parents carried on with their lives afterwards. Not until we started seeing birth parents at the Post-Adoption Centre did I really stop to think how they must perceive social workers and what, from their perspective, adoption looks like. So perhaps a good place to start is with some views birth mothers have expressed to us, as a way of trying to get somewhere near the shoes they stand in:

116

I never saw my social worker after my baby was taken away. She phoned me once, but it wasn't me she was interested in – it was helping the adopters become parents.

My social worker was very kind, but she had no idea of how I would feel afterwards. She said to go back to work and try to pretend it never happened. She didn't realise the pain was so great I could hardly get out of bed in the morning. And not only mental pain – my breasts hurt, my whole body ached for my baby.

Birthdays are the worst. I think about my son a lot of the time, but on his birthday I long to know where and how he is, what he looks like, what he's doing. When he was seven I wrote to the agency asking if I could have news of him – just to know he was alive and well – but the social worker said they couldn't interfere in the adopters' lives by going back and asking. I felt as though I didn't really exist. My son had appeared on earth and had a life out there, but I had no part in it.

I couldn't have kept my daughter – I didn't even want to. I wasn't ready to be a parent, I was appalled at the thought. Adoption was the only possible solution – but I felt so guilty. I think the social worker thought I was an easy case because I just went along with everything and was so sure I was doing the right thing. But the guilt was awful – and it has never gone away. I wanted so much to explain to the adoptive parents, but no one suggested I should meet them and I didn't know you could. Now I long to see my daughter and explain to her. Also to know she is alright, and doesn't hate me.

Those are not unusual things for birth mothers to say. At the Post-Adoption Centre we hear such views and feelings expressed over and over again: pain, grief, guilt and the longing to know what has happened – whether the decision was the right one – is the child alive and well?

Of course there are variations. Some people would rather go on trying to forget, not letting the child become too real for them. At the other extreme, some people would ask nothing better than to claim the child back. But there is high overall agreement on a middle ground: what a lot of birth parents would like is periodic information.

Many mothers have spoken of the void in their lives, which marriage, other children, successful careers, cannot fill. They speak too of the torment of wondering whether their son was in the disaster at the football stadium at Hillsborough, their daughter in the ferry at Zeebrugge; was it their child knocked down by a motorist they read about in the newspaper? The age was the same, and they *think* the agency told them the adoptive father was a teacher, like this child's father . . . .

We should not be surprised at this, though we may never have realised how lasting the torment can be. Women may have been told to 'go away and put it all behind them' and many felt they should 'get over it', like a bereavement. But bereft as they may have been, there was no dead baby, no funeral, no ceremony for them. The child was very much alive, handed over to parents who had longed for just such a baby. Each mother knew her child was out there somewhere, but that she would never again have news of them, or see how they fared in life.

Good-bye, or au revoir?

Not, that is, until 1975. Then the law was changed, but changed with no reference to birth parents because they had no voice, no public face – often, some felt, no real existence. The Natural Parents' Support Group had not yet been founded, and how could legislators have consulted these three quarters of a million women, few of whom had never identified themselves to anyone else at all? Society was, and still is, in the gradual process of changing enough to accept single parenthood and non-marital status births without stigma, but even now it takes a brave woman to announce that she not only bore a child out of wedlock but also parted with it for adoption. If she is not censured for the one, she is likely to be so for the other.

When the law changed, it radically altered the way that parents who were parting with a child had to view that action. Before, it was 'good-bye' and facing up to a period, perhaps a lifetime, of grieving for a child who was permanently lost. Now parents know that in 18 years' time that child will have the right to know who they were, and to trace them if she or he so chooses. Some fix their sights on that day, and carry on in the belief and hope that it really is only 'au revoir'. Others say, 'Well, I'll deal with it when it comes, though at the moment it is not what I want'. But, whatever their feelings, they cannot ignore the fact that adoption has already become in one sense 'open' – or at least open-ended.

This has many implications for birth parents, not only at the time of parting with the child but also later on. Adopted people are increasingly seeking out birth relatives, most of whom had not thought anything like that could ever happen. The meetings are often highly emotional, stirring up depths of feelings for which people are unprepared. Birth mothers in particular may feel in emotional turmoil when a son or daughter traces them. So many mixed feelings come surging back from the past – about the child's father, about their own parents, about the experience of the pregnancy and the birth, and the loss of the parting. Alongside that, they are trying to reconcile the image of an adult man or woman with the baby they remember. They may also be trying to handle this event in relation to a husband, children, their parents, who may or may not have known already of the existence of the child. Small wonder they talk of 'not knowing whether they are coming or going', 'living on a volcano', 'being in a daze', and report things like being sent home from work because they are accomplishing nothing.

Exchanging information
One way of trying to prepare for such an event is for those involved to learn what they can about each other before they actually meet – by exchanges of letters and photographs, for example, or by whatever other means can help put some reality into what may have been 30 years of fantasy. Better still would surely be to feed some reality in over the years, so that a meeting, if it occurs, does not come as the earth-shattering event it often is. A periodic exchange of information over the years could go a long way towards helping people prepare for meeting again as adults.

In discussing such a possibility in birth mothers' groups, most agreed that they would prefer to have information lodged at the agency, to ask for if and when they wanted, rather than having it sent to them out of the blue. Many women said there had been periods of their life when they would not have felt able to cope with receiving news, or before they had told a partner or subsequent children when the unexpected arrival of information could have been difficult to handle. On the other hand, to know that they could approach the agency when they did feel ready, and to learn that the adoptive parents had left news for them, would have made an enormous difference. Most also felt they would have been glad to update the picture of themselves the adopters had been given, with news of developments in their own lives and relationships.

One fear that adoptive parents sometimes have is that periodic news may not be enough, and that knowing only a little will be frustrating for a mother, who might then want to press for more, or for a meeting. This could of course be true, and people rarely know in advance how they will feel in given circumstances. Most of the women in the groups, however, thought they would have found comfort in having a little knowledge, while still recognising that there was no way they could or would want to upset the adoption. There is a lot of fantasy about birth mothers behaving irresponsibly, and perhaps 'snatching children back' or disrupting their lives in some way. In fact, most of the mothers of the past who accepted adoption did so as the only *responsible* way of providing adequately for their child. They feel hurt and angry if it is implied that they would not continue to put their child's needs first, or that they would abuse the trust shown to them in allowing them periodic information.

The very fact that access to information has to be 'allowed' by both adopters and agency highlights the imbalance of power in the so-called 'adoption triangle'. This has frequently been commented on in the groups run by the Post-Adoption Centre. Women feel they continue to be viewed as immature, perhaps irresponsible, as naughty or even wicked 'girls' or, just as patronisingly, as 'birth mums'. The fact that they either made the greatest sacrifice they could for their child's sake, or else were given no choice at all by their own parents or by society, is often overlooked. So, too, is the fact that most of them have grown into perfectly ordinary responsible citizens, mothers, partners, who cannot in any way be distinguished from the rest of the population, even enough to obtain their opinions on adoption.

Another argument in favour of making information available over the years is that, far from making a mother feel she wants to take back her child, it can emphasise for her how far the child actually belongs to another family. Following membership of a birth mothers' group, more than one woman felt strengthened enough to approach the placement agency for updated news. Where the agency agreed to approach the adopters, they tended to meet with a positive response and the birth mother was able to learn something about how her child was developing. For one woman in particular, this was a watershed as it gave her both reassurance and the ability finally to separate herself from the past. She realised that the baby she had been mourning was now a happy, much-loved little girl who was fully established as a member of her adoptive family. The birth mother felt sad but freed, and went off to take a new direction in her life in a way she had hitherto felt unable to do because so much emotional energy had been tied up in fighting her grief, anger and guilt.

Some parents feel the balance of power is so unequal, and their rights and needs have been so little recognised, that they have set out to crack the system and trace their adopted child. A few have said they would have felt less need to do this is if the agency had been willing to give or obtain information. It was the fact of being treated as though they were tiresome or untrustworthy adolescents which fired them to decide to take matters into their own hands. Several who have been seen at the Centre have succeeded in tracing the child, but if he or she was under 18, and sometimes if they were older, have decided to wait before making contact. This was partly to give the young person the chance to start a search themselves, so the parent would know contact would be welcome, but also because some found that knowing their child was alive and well, and in some cases having actually seen them from afar and being convinced of their wellbeing, had been enough to be going on with. Disrupting their lives was the last thing the parents wanted. It would seem very possible that an organised exchange of information could have served the same purpose and avoided these birth parents feeling they had to go to the lengths involved to find their child.

Greater openness – contact throughout childhood

For some parents, it may be possible to go further than an exchange of information and to contemplate a far greater openness, involving actual meetings throughout childhood. After all, there are many precedents for the successful rearing of someone else's child, with contact, in West Indian and other black communities, and it is time the white world looked at how this works and tried to learn from it. There is also evidence of fully open adoption working well in New Zealand, and many examples in this country of grandparents staying in touch. However, for parents to have contact is a potentially difficult undertaking and depends heavily on all parties being very clear about each other's role and intentions, and having complete trust in each other. One of the reasons fostering can be so difficult is because there are two sets of parents actively in the picture, and the acceptance of the role of each is sometimes lacking or undermined.

Children need security, clear boundaries, and undivided loyalties in their early years. If birth parents can accept this and, having parted with their child for adoption, acknowledge that they are no longer the active parents in any sense, then there is no reason why contact should not be workable. Adoptive parents would also need the confidence to act fully as the child's parents, and some might find this difficult in the presence of the birth mother or father. An adoptive parent needs to believe: 'I am Susan's mother/father. I therefore have the right to guide and control her, to tell her off, to care for her when she has measles, and to expect her to turn first to me. But her birth mother also has a close interest and concern, and this is important for her, and I can encourage it.'

The birth parent needs to believe: 'I am *not* Susan's mother in that way, so I do not have the right to do any of those things. But I *do* have a close interest and concern, and as long as it does not undermine her relationship with her day-to-day parents, I can express it.'

The child needs to be clear: 'I am Susan Brown, not Susan Smith, and I belong to the Brown household. But I know Jane Smith cares a lot about me because I grew in her tummy and I care about her, and that is OK by everybody.'

Put like that, it is obvious that the relationship is much more like that of a godparent or favourite aunt than a second mother, which it is much harder to be or to accept.

The opportunity for splitting people, and playing one off against the other, is of course always present for adopted children. How many adoptive parents have flung at them: 'My *real* mother would let me' or words to that effect? If the birth mother is a known person, a child can easily try to capitalise on the situation, and the adults have to remain mature and firm to counteract this. One birth mother who had been in contact with her daughter sporadically over the years found the girl turning to her more in adolescence, complaining of the way her parents tried to control her. The birth mother was clear-minded and strong about this and regularly sent the girl home without colluding with her, in firm support of the adoptive parents. It may not always have been easy to do this, particularly if the birth mother would have handled the initial situation differently herself, but in this case it made a continuing relationship possible and was far more helpful than encouraging a split in the adoptive family.

One kind of adoption where more openness might really help is transracial adoption. Groups of transracially-adopted adults meeting at the Centre have highlighted their sense of isolation in their adoptive family. Most were extremely vague about their origins, and some people of mixed parentage counselled at the Centre did not even know which parent had been black, or what his or her racial origins were. Updated information, or possible contact with family members or even parents, could make a considerable difference to children growing up in this way, and to the birth parents too.

Contested adoptions

All this discussion relates, as will have been obvious, to parents who agree or who have agreed to the adoption of their child, however reluctantly or heartbrokenly. The situation may be very different when a child has been removed from parents through the courts, for neglect or ill-treatment, and is then placed for adoption. Such adoptions form an increasingly large percentage of placements nowadays, and the attitudes of those involved may not be at all the same as in the baby adoptions of the past. Adopters may well feel angry and condemnatory of parents who have abused a child, and the birth parents may be even more consumed by guilt, anger and shame, expressed perhaps as violence or depression. In these cases, there would need to be very careful consideration about the wisdom of continuing contact, and in many cases of ill-treatment the court would probably be awarding an adoption order to ensure that the child was protected.

However, that does not mean to say that 'openness' in terms of information should not be considered. In some ways, it can be argued that there is a greater, rather than a lesser, need for it. The guilt of the birth parents is often so great that they fear they have done lasting damage to a child. To be able to learn periodically how the child is progressing could make a big difference to their ability to carry on with their lives. There can be few more terrible things to live with than the knowledge of having abused a child. It would seem only humane over the years to allow parents once in a while to be given some reassurance about the child's progress. They will be suffering enough torment without being denied what comfort may be available. And often they are people who have had least in life anyway, both in material terms and in the way of satisfying or even adequate relationships. Many abusing parents were themselves abused or deprived. Their lives are often a form of continuing punishment. Need they be made more so?

The other side of the coin is that adoptive parents, as well as the child, can benefit from a periodical update of information about the birth parents, if the latter are willing to give it. People do grow and mature, and circumstances can change. It would be sad, for instance, to let a child grow up with an image of a deprived, isolated young mother driven to the end of her tether and ill-treating the child, when perhaps this woman has found a stable partner, settled down, and is doing a good job of bringing up other children.

For the birth parents to be enabled, even encouraged, to lodge information with the agency would have a number of benefits. Just the fact that anyone thought it worthwhile to receive progress reports could help their self-esteem – and nobody is all bad. It would also mean they kept in touch with the agency and might, as time passed, be able to accept help or counselling for themselves. In the early days of a child's removal, the anger and guilt is often too great to allow the parent to accept help from the department which is involved. That highlights the need for independent counselling or support centres but it may also be possible that, later, the parents can in fact be helped by the original department and this would be facilitated by the exchange of information.

In fact, 'openness' can start from the word go, in small ways. However abusive or neglectful, birth parents are the holders of an enormous amount of information which is vitally important both to the child and the adopters. It can be a healing process for the parents to be enabled to compile records of the child's past – photograph albums, list of events, tape-recorded memories, birthday cards, health histories, and so on, and to pass these on to the adopters. One mother we know of was greatly helped by doing all this over a period of time, ending with making a personal tape-recording for her son when he grew older. In this, she told him how sad she was that she had not been able to be a good enough mother to him; that she had tried, but had not known how, and lacked the support she needed. She reminded him of some of the good times they had had together, and she told him she loved him, and always would. She said how she hoped he was growing up happily in his new family. It was a simple, very moving message, and could mean a great deal to the boy and to his adoptive parents. Many birth parents could be helped to do something like this, and to express some of the love and the sorrow they feel, instead of being left thinking that all they had been able to show the child had been anger or abuse.

Conclusion

It is clear that this kind of work has implications for resources, notably staff time. In the past we have all underestimated the amount of sensitive work that must go into the successful transplanting of a child. More is needed than we realised, even with babies, if the needs of *all* parties, including birth relatives, are to be considered. When we are transplanting older children, as so often we are nowadays – and often they are damaged plants – the work involved is much greater and the making of an adoption order cannot be seen as the end of the road. For the family, life is only just beginning. And for the birth parents, who have made, or have had made for them, the hardest decision any human being has to make, the road ahead is a rough and uphill one. Instead of punishing them yet more, should we not be finding ways of helping them to live with their loss, and maybe even to go on contributing, in however small a way, to the success of the adoption?

LOOKING BACK OVER A LIFETIME – THE NEW ZEALAND EXPERIENCE OF ACCESS TO RECORDS AND ADULT REUNIONS

9 Adult adoption information in New Zealand - key differences from England and Wales

Audrey Mullender

Of those countries which previously had closed records, England and Wales moved to open up birth records at a relatively early date. Adult adopted people of 18 and over have had rights to birth records information since the 1975 Children Act was implemented in November 1976. In Scotland, adopted adults have always had access to their records and the research by Triseliotis[1] into the use of this provision was a major factor in changing the law south of the border. Campaigners in New Zealand used the success of this change to go one step further and seek rights for birth parents also. They eventually succeeded in getting an Act passed – the Adult Adoption Information Act, 1985 – which does indeed cover both adult adopted people and birth parents. To get it accepted by the policy makers, however, other relatives had to be left out (now becoming a new focus of campaigning of which the Government is aware) and a com-promise had to be accepted which has proved to be probably the major shortcoming of the legislation. This is the provision whereby either party – a birth parent of a person adopted before 1 March 1986 or an adult adopted person at any date – can place a veto on access to information which would identify them. The key strength of the New Zealand legislation, as compared with ours, is that it has given greater recognition to the needs of birth parents.

The New Zealand 1985 Adult Adoption Information Act, then, has recognised birth parents by giving them the right, within the constraints imposed by vetoes, to trace their adopted children. The contact register introduced by the 1989 Children Act here does not go anywhere near this far, and it is to be hoped that it will be only a staging post on the way towards a wider-scale change. What the New Zealand birth parent applies for is identifying information about their son or daughter. This includes the right to be told if their child has subsequently died and whatever other information about them the Director General of Social Welfare thinks fit to release, or that their son or daughter (if aged 19 or more) has placed

129

an endorsement on identifying information and the date when this will expire.

Reluctance of birth parents to use the legislation

Despite having the right to information, far fewer birth parents than adopted people apply: 2385 birth parents to the end of July 1989, as against 10,205 adopted people (official statistics from the Department of Social Welfare contained in a personal letter). The comparison is, however, distorted by the fact that a far higher number of adopted people have applied for information in New Zealand than in other countries with comparable laws: within the first eight months after the Act came into force, adopted people representing 10 per cent of all orders made since 1910 had applied for certificates; even excluding all family and step-parent adoptions, this represents about a fifth of all those in the 20 to 40 year old age group.[2]

The most likely reason for birth parents' reluctance to apply is that they feel they have no right to reappear in their son or daughter's life. They gave up their child never expecting to see him or her again and feel they would now be intruding. Significantly, however, thousands wrote in to the Department of Social Welfare when the law changed, saying that they were willing to have contact if the adopted person requested it. There have, by the time of writing, been an estimated 8,500 reunions, half of which have led to continuing contact, and only six serious complaints about the working of the Act (figures from Keith Griffith in conference presentation).

A further reason for birth mothers' reluctance to initiate contact may be that they have often been left submissive and lacking in self-esteem by their experiences. Jeff Field of Auckland University (personal meeting; see also chapter 10) believes that they feel powerless and blamed, trapped in a victim status. It would take a strong drive of anger or of collective support to lift a woman out of those disabling feelings and into a process of individual and perhaps wider change. Field has found positive differences in the well-being of birth mothers who have had a reunion as against those who have not. Dominick's research[3] suggests also that meetings, after initially bringing birth parents' grief to the fore, then help them to get over it.

Vetoes

Either party – a birth parent or an adopted person aged at least 19 (the age of majority being 20 in New Zealand) – can request the Registrar-General to 'endorse' the original entry of the birth in the official records which places a veto on access to identifying information about themselves and, hence, prevents their being contacted by that means. The law requires that they be offered optional counselling before this is done and, if they accept the counselling, they must request the endorsement afresh thereafter.

The largest number of vetoes were placed in the early months after the law changed. In the first seven months, 816 were placed by adopted people and 2626 by birth parents, all except 41 of the latter by birth mothers (official statistics from the Department of Social Welfare contained in a personal letter). Since then, they have gradually tailed away (30 and 40 by the two groups respectively in January to July 1989; source as above). Whereas only birth parents of people adopted before 1 March 1986 can place vetoes – so, in their case, the provision is time-limited – adopted people will always retain the right to place an apparent veto on being contacted by one or both birth parents, as specified by them. I use the word 'apparent' in relation to vetoes, because the possibilities of circumventing vetoes have proved to be very great, especially for those with access to people able to advise them what to do (notably others who have followed such a course in the past). Vetoes do not, therefore, guarantee anonymity and the right to place them may lead only to a false sense of security.

Vetoes placed by either party can be removed, at their request, at any time or will automatically expire either after 10 years, unless renewed, or on the death of the person who placed the veto. Even so, if the death occurs after an application for information has been dealt with, the person who has sought information will not be recontacted and told that they can now have the information they desire. Hence, they will only get it if they themselves happen to find out about the death. Where there is no veto placed by the adopted person, and if their current identity is known to the Department of Social Welfare and they can be contacted by a social worker without 'undue effort', then they are asked whether they are willing to have their name and address revealed to their birth parent. They will always retain this double safeguard against unwelcome contact.

The provision of a double safeguard means that the rights of birth parents are not fully equal to those of adopted people, even in New

Zealand, because they have two hurdles they may fall at rather than one. It was introduced as an attempt to soften the blow for anyone who does not know they were adopted, although there is no evidence to suggest that this news comes as less of a bombshell from a social worker than from one's own birth parent.

The mechanism of prior contact from an Adult Adoption Information worker is no more effective than the veto in guaranteeing anonymity. The existence of both may, therefore, lend a still greater sense of false security. Ironically, if the adopted person cannot be found by the Department of Social Welfare, the courts' interpretation of the precise wording of the Act has been that the information identifying them can be released. Since birth parents have often proved far more effective in locating their children than the Department, this has led to additional reunions taking place.

Adoption support groups in New Zealand and campaigning groups of birth mothers are unanimous in condemning vetoes. They have caused untold heartache to those encountering them and can also make matters worse for those placing them in that they may remain 'stuck' in an unresolved emotional state. The message emerging very strongly from New Zealand is that we should on no account contemplate the introduction of vetoes in Britain.

Counselling

In New Zealand, a person whose birth certificate is released in a form which identifies one or both parents (that is, either with no vetoes or with one only, where the other parent is also recorded), and who was adopted before 1 March 1986, is required to receive counselling from an approved counsellor. For those adopted after 28 February 1986, when they reach the age of majority and if they wish to exercise their rights under this legislation, counselling will be optional and the birth certificate will be received either through the post or from a counsellor, as preferred by the adopted person.

As in Britain, the implication of counselling is that the adopted person needs to think very carefully about the possible repercussions for themselves and others if they are contemplating trying to establish contact with a birth parent after so many years. Unlike the situation in Britain, approved counsellors include not only social workers but also independent counsellors and employees of approved independent organisations (often a member of the adoption triad and frequently linked with an adoption support group). After the counselling has taken place, as in Britain, the counsellor has no right to withhold the birth certificate.

If the adopted person is permanently resident outside New Zealand, they are posted a copy of their original birth certificate and the address of the Director of Social Welfare. This differs markedly from recent practice covering adoptions in England and Wales, which has required any person living overseas to return for compulsory counselling to take place in this country before the birth certificate can be released. This has caused great distress amongst people adopted in Britain but now living elsewhere who cannot afford to return but who are desperate for information. It has also evoked considerable anger amongst approved counsellors in New Zealand and elsewhere that they are not considered 'good enough', as they see it, to provide the counselling themselves. Fortunately, this provision has been changed under the 1989 Children Act and it will in future be acceptable to receive counselling in the country of domicile.

Since the adopted person is an adult, the involvement of a social worker can be controversial, certainly where it is imposed rather than simply made available by legislation. There are two aspects to this debate: the provision of counselling to the person seeking adult adoption information, and the question of whether there should be an intermediary between birth parent and adopted person when re-establishing contact. Keith Griffith,[4] a prominent adoption law campaigner in New Zealand, argues strongly (personal conversation and unpublished conference presentation) that the continuing protection of someone once they are adult by counsellors and intermediaries – and the existence of this different principle in law just for adoption and not, for example, in the field of marital disputes – is a contentious human rights issue. The matter is even thornier elsewhere: in the State of Victoria in Australia, there is alleged to be an eight to 12-year waiting list for receiving birth certificates, with counsellors apparently wielding considerable power over adopted people whom they consider need long programmes of counselling before the information can safely be handed over. Although it does make counselling mandatory, the law both in New Zealand and Britain specifically denies counsellors the right to withhold a birth certificate.

Despite debating the necessity of making counselling compulsory, even on a time-limited basis, all seem agreed that it is perfectly

133

reasonable and helpful to have counsellors available if requested. On the other hand, the policy-makers may have been concerned to protect the interests of birth parents whose lives could be radically affected by a retroactive change in legislation. In that case, the question becomes one of what possible influence a counsellor can have over someone who has already determined on a course of action, however dramatic its effects may be. And the anecdotal evidence from Adult Adoption Information workers in the Department of Social Welfare seems to be that, in fact, adopted people tend to handle reunions with their own birth parents in a far more appropriate way than would an intermediary who does not share either their personal experiences or their personality type.

The issue of an intermediary crops up because either party, or an adoptive parent, can ask an Adult Adoption Information worker to make contact with the other party on their behalf. The worker can, however, decline and many encourage the adopted person to make their own approach. To delegate such an emotionally charged occasion as a reunion to a proxy, they argue, is like missing one's own wedding. Added to this, if they are met with a rejection, the adopted person will never know whether they would have met with a more successful response had they gone in person and handled it differently or, at least, not given their parent the chance of backing out.

If the worker does agree to act in the capacity of intermediary, the legislation requires them to ask if the person is willing to be contacted and how ('under what circumstances'), and to report back. If the person being contacted is a birth parent, the social worker is to tell them of their rights to place a veto on information about themselves in respect of any other child they may have had adopted, and if the person contacted is an adult who was adopted they are to be told that they can still veto contact from their other birth parent whether or not they accept it on this first approach.

Adoption support groups

As I have described elsewhere,[5] Adult Adoption Information workers often see their role as one of giving advice on the options rather than counselling in any therapeutic sense. They try to see adopted people as adults who are capable of reaching their own decisions. A further part of the reason for the difference in approach is that self-help groups in New Zealand take on the major emotional support role for many people, and can do so over a much longer period than it would be possible or appropriate for a counsellor to offer.

Most towns and cities in New Zealand have an adoption support group, which is open to all members of the adoption triad. In the early days, the consumers played a key role in advising activists and the Department of Social Welfare what changes were needed and in lobbying for legal reform. Groups now play an especially important role for those who are about to try and make contact, or have just done so, or who have received a veto. Anyone experiencing an emotionally-charged situation related to adoption can receive tremendous help from such a group and some people continue to attend over a long period of time. Amongst these are some who become the mainstay of the group and remain in it mainly to offer support to newcomers whose experiences they recognise as echoing their own. The group in Christchurch, for example, has members who helped establish it ten years ago and many others who have joined since. At one particular meeting attended by the author, there were 27 people present. All were women, apart from the partner of one young adopted woman and one Adult Adoption Information worker who is also a birth father. (There had been 44 attenders at the last meeting but numbers had fallen because another group had just started in nearby Rangiora with 20 members.) In the Christchurch group, even with 27 present, it took three hours just to work round the circle and hear everyone's story, as well as offering verbal support and advice to those who needed it.

One of the most noticeable phenomena at this meeting was that it was not always another adopted person or another birth or adoptive parent who offered the support. Often, a different member of the adoption triad from the one whose story held the floor could see the situation from a fresh perspective and could offer words of wisdom. A young woman who had encountered a veto, for example, was helped to reflect on how her birth mother might be feeling by other birth mothers present, as well as being given the boost of hearing from other people who had circumvented vetoes. Another young woman, attending her first meeting, had actually recently placed a veto. It was clear that she had done so because of a generally confused and unhappy situation in which she could not face any further emotional turmoil at that stage. There was every hope that the whole group would, over time, be able to help her develop emotionally until she felt more comfortable with who and what she was. The existence of the veto mechanism, in fact, seemed to have encouraged her to hide behind it rather than facing up to her own need to move on.

Conclusion

New Zealand has developed some key differences in its treatment of adult adopted people and their birth parents from the situation we in Britain are accustomed to. Not all of these have been positive. Vetoes have been overwhelmingly reckoned a disaster and we are urged not to contemplate them here in our legislation. The counselling role, in a situation of greater complexity and keener campaigning, has given rise to more controversy in New Zealand than in Britain and has been interpreted differently. Notably, members of the adoption triad have been encouraged to take action on their own behalf, rather than using the social worker as an intermediary, and to seek continuing support from adoption self-help groups rather than from professionals.

The biggest advance in New Zealand compared to Britain lies in the rights accorded to birth parents. Though still subject to some limitations (in the form both of legislative safeguards and personal reluctance to come forward) these represent a social and ideological shift in recognising birth parents as full members of the adoption triad who can no longer be ignored. Hearing them speaking out, individually in programmes on New Zealand television, and collectively in adoption support groups and through birth mother campaigning groups, one is struck not only by the length of time they have remained silent in Britain but also by the degree to which hearing their voice could cause the next radical shift in thinking about adoption – by opening it up at all stages of the process. If we no longer needed to shut out birth parents as a threat to their children or to adopters, then secrecy and closed records, and perhaps even stranger adoption itself, could be at an end. It must also be acknowledged that, both in New Zealand and in Britain, the views and interests of birth fathers have yet to enter fully into the frame and, in Britain, the parents of older children placed for adoption from care will raise somewhat different issues.

Organisations like the Family Rights Group are assisting this last group to be heard and are supporting the Grandparents' Federation in arguing the cause of other birth relatives with an important contribution to make. Against the backdrop of the Adoption Law review, now is a very appropriate time for us to start listening.

References

1 Triseliotis J *In search of origins* Routledge & Kegan Paul, 1973.

2 Iwanek M 'A study of open adoption placements: the experiences over a period of time of 17 adoptive families and 14 birth mothers who had entered into an open adoption arrangement' Lower Hutt, New Zealand: Department of Social Welfare (unpublished), 1987.

3 Dominick C *Early contact in adoption: contact between birth mothers and adoptive parents at the time of and after the adoption* Research Series no 10, Wellington: Department of Social Welfare, 1988.

4 Griffith K C *Adoption procedures, documentation and statistics. New Zealand, 1881-1981. 100 Years* Wellington: published by the author 1981, and *100 Years of New Zealand adoption 1881-1981* (unpublished), 1981.

5 Mullender A 'Adoption in New Zealand – a British perspective' *Adoption & Fostering* 14 4, 1990.

10 Views of New Zealand birth mothers on search and reunion

Jeff Field

The practice of strangers providing a house and upbringing for children who have for some reason been let go by their birth parents has a long history among New Zealanders of European origin.[1] Completely confidential and closed adoptions were particularly common in New Zealand in the decades immediately following World War II. With the implementation of the 1985 Adult Adoption Information Act in 1986 in New Zealand, birth parents and adopted people who were separated at least 20 years ago have begun to have an opportunity to make contact with one another. Since 1986, over 10,000 adopted people have applied for their birth certificates and about 3,000 birth mothers have sought information about their relinquished children. (New Zealand Department of Social Welfare: unpublished data.) Possible reasons for such a disparity in application rates by adopted people and birth mothers will be discussed in this paper, which reports findings on the feelings of a nationwide sample of New Zealand birth mothers about their experiences either before or after reunion with children relinquished between 20 and 30 years earlier. The birth mothers participating in this study wanted, if possible, to have some kind of renewed contact with their children and they had taken at least an initial step towards that goal.

Aims of the study

For birth mothers involved in the closed and secretive adoption procedures that operated in New Zealand and Australia until about 15 years ago, it is widely acknowledged that there may have been serious impediments to their grieving the losses experienced around

---

A very brief summary of this study has already appeared in *Adoption & Fostering* 14 3, 1990. More detailed discussion of the statistical analyses of the survey component of this study is available in an unpublished paper by the author.

the time of the relinquishment.[2] In particular, it is arguable that these closed adoption practices have left many birth mothers in a psychological state where they have not been able to 'say a final goodbye' and have been left wondering whether one day they will somehow experience renewed contact with their relinquished son or daughter. Lack of information about the well-being of the child may often generate continuing uncertainty about the effects of their relinquishment and lead to concerns about the child's health and development, which may augment feelings of guilt about the adoption.[3]

These suggestions about the possible impairment of the grieving process and the long-term guilt feelings experienced by birth mothers can be further explored by comparing women who have been able to have a reunion with their relinquished child with those who have not yet had a reunion. Previous surveys of birth mothers in Australia[4] and New Zealand[5] have not been able to assess the adjustment of mothers to possible reunions with their sons or daughters. A general main objective of this study was to compare the emotional well-being of mothers who had already experienced a reunion with that of mothers who were awaiting the possibility of such a reunion.

The findings discussed here specifically address three issues. First, the significance to birth mothers of the availability of information about the life and well-being of the children that they relinquished for adoption was examined. Earlier investigators have suggested that the availability of such information, which may range in nature from non-identifying details to direct personal contact, is very important for the long-term adjustment of many birth mothers.[6] A second objective was to examine the experiences of women who had been able to have renewed contact with their children. Both individual differences and general trends in birth mothers' feelings were explored. To clarify some of these individual differences, a second part of this study comprised in-depth interviews with a sub-sample of the surveyed birth mothers. The interviews not only enabled a more detailed assessment to be made of mothers' feelings about the search and reunion processes, but also provided data on the third issue of interest: birth mothers' views on the age restriction, veto, and counselling provisions of the present adoption legislation in New Zealand.

Survey and interview procedures

The sample for the survey was recruited from the total of 2,024 mothers who approached the Department of Social Welfare in New Zealand for identifying information about their relinquished children between September 1986 and March 1989. The research section of the Department of Social Welfare mailed these women a letter asking for their written consent to participate in possible future research concerned with adoption. Written consent was obtained from 551 birth mothers. It was after these events that the present investigator obtained the permission of the Department to make these 551 women the target of this questionnaire survey. A copy of the questionnaire was mailed out to all potential respondents by the Department of Social Welfare. A total of 444 usable qustionnaires were returned to the researcher which gave an analysable return rate of 80 per cent.

The questionnaire was comprised of 82 pre-coded questions about: pregnancy and relinquishment experiences; general life changes; psychological well-being (as measured by the General Health Questionnaire [GHQ-28] and a short self-esteem scale); intensity of negative and positive feelings about adoption events; perceived availability of emotional support; and any reunion experiences. Examples of the positive and negative affect and the emotional support questions are given in Table 1. Changes in feeling about adoption events were assessed by asking mothers about the six categories of affect in Table 1 with regard to the months immediately after the relinquishment, immediately after any renewed contact and in the last few months. Women who had experienced some direct personal contact with their daughter or son since relinquishment were asked whether they had received any counselling, or special group support, before or after the reunion, and how prepared they had felt in retrospect for the event. Their frequency of present contact, overall satisfaction with the reunion, and any reasons for dissatisfaction, were also explored.

For the second part of the study 21 birth mothers who lived in the general Auckland region were interviewed. About 80 Auckland birth mothers indicated their willingness to be interviewed on their survey forms. In selecting mothers for interview, only a qualitative attempt was made to match their distributions of age, educational back-ground, and time since reunion characteristics to those of the survey

Table 1

Questions concerning the intensity of feelings about adoption events and the availability of support

20   Now we would like you to think about your feelings about the adoption events in recent months. In the last few months to what degree have you been feeling ... ? (circle a number for each feeling)

	Not at all	A little	Moder-ately	A lot	Totally
A sense of loss	1	2	3	4	5
A sense of sadness	1	2	3	4	5
A sense of guilt	1	2	3	4	5

21   In the last few months to what degree have you been feeling ... ? (circle a number for each feeling)

	Not at all	A little	Moder-ately	A lot	Totally
A sense of relief	1	2	3	4	5
A sense of calm	1	2	3	4	5
A sense of joy	1	2	3	4	5

22   During the last few months how often have you felt that help of an emotional kind was available when you needed it?

Not at all	Very rarely	Some of the time	Very often	All of the time
1	2	3	4	5

23   During the last few months how often have you felt that you could talk freely and express your feelings to others about the adoption events when you needed to do so?

Not at all	Very rarely	Some of the time	Very often	All of the time
1	2	3	4	5

sample. Eight of the interviewees had not renewed contact, while 13 had. Four female psychology graduates who were trained in clinical interviewing skills carried out the interviews at a time and place chosen by the birth parents. The interviewers transcribed each of their own interviews within 24 hours of their completion. The interview content was semi-structured and covered the following areas:

1 feelings experienced during the search period leading up to, but not including, the first contact between the adopted person and the birth mother

2 feelings experienced during any initial reunion and since that time

3 feelings about the relationship with the adopted daughter or son

4 feelings about the relationship with the adoptive parents

5 opinions about the present legislated procedures of an age minimum of 20 years for renewed contact initiated by one party and veto provisions for each party.

Characteristics of the sample

Before describing some selected findings from this research, important background features of the sample of birth mothers need to be outlined. These research findings are limited to birth mothers who had experienced completely confidential and closed adoptions, but who now wanted to have some kind of contact with their relinquished children and who had taken at least an initial step towards that goal. The results of this study cannot be generalised to all birth mothers who relinquished children during the same era in New Zealand and the question of whether this sample was biased toward women who have coped more, or less, effectively with their relinquishments is not easily answerable. Nevertheless, it was evident from the range of open-ended comments included by mothers in their questionnaire responses that the sample was representative of a broad range of coping levels among birth mothers.

About 80 per cent of the mothers had relinquished children between 20 and 30 years earlier, and about 80 per cent of reunions had taken place within the previous two years. Two hundred and six of the mothers had not had any renewed contact, while 238 had been able to renew personal contact with their son or daughter. (These two groups will sometimes be referred to as the pre- and post-reunion birth mothers in this paper.) Sixty-four per cent of mothers surveyed had relinquished a child when they were 19 years or younger. The educational backgrounds of the women had a distribution that was typical of New Zealand women of their age range. The sub-sample of 21 birth mothers whose interview results are reported here ranged in age from 36 to 51 years. Eleven had relinquished sons and 10 had relinquished daughters.

The recollections of the majority of mothers about their pregnancy and relinquishment experiences indicated feelings of a lack of choice and very little in the way of socio-emotional support, both around the time of those events and often also in the decades that followed. About 100 women included detailed, personal experiences in the 'open comments' section of the questionnaire that vividly supported these recollections. The pre- and post-reunion sub-groups did not differ significantly on key background factors such as perceived emotional support at the time of relinquishment, educational background, or frequency of negative life events.

Searching and the importance of information

Examination of the interview transcripts and open-ended questionnaire comments yielded three very common, inter-related elements in birth mothers' search for information. The first was that many had spent a long time in what could loosely be called a search phase. For example, it was quite common for mothers to get some non-identifying information and not make any more active search efforts for a long while thereafter. There were marked individual differences in the apparent reasons for such delays, but the important point seems to be that birth mothers were often reluctant to push matters.

The second common element in the search process was the frequent sense of uncertainty, frustration and powerlessness expressed by the birth mothers:

I would do anything to find out, because I have to have a name, even if I don't meet her. I have to know because it is too long. Twenty years is too long not to know that information. It gives you back a bit of power because you are powerless for too long, and just having the surname is a bit of power. Even if I don't act on it, it gives me something back.

143

The feelings of uncertainty and powerlessness sometimes related to not knowing what to do to get more information.

These two common features of birth mothers' behaviour – their reluctance to push matters and their sense of uncertainty – may partly explain why, in the time since the implementation of the Adult Adoption Information Act in New Zealand, applications for information from adopted people have outnumbered those from birth parents by almost four to one. Preston[7] examined many letters from birth mothers who want to leave a record of willingness to make contact, but who do not wish to make a formal application under the Act. She says tht the most commonly cited reasons for not initiating an approach directly are:

1 Many remember that, at the time of giving consent to adoption, they swore on the Bible that they would never attempt to find their child. A change in the law does not enable these women to forswear that oath.

2 Anxiety that the adopted person may never have been told of the adoption and that telling him/her may be psychologically damaging.

3 Fear that the adoptive family may feel the birth parent is trying to usurp their place in the adopted person's life and affections.

4 Feelings of unworthiness relating to the stigma of unwed parenthood and the guilt from having given their child away.

The third general, and very well-known, feature of the search process is that eventually receiving identifying or non-identifying information can be crucial to removing a lot of the strong uncertainty facing birth mothers for decades after a closed adoption. For example, when one interviewed mother found out her son's name and that he lived in Hong Kong, she said:

> Yes, I think it's quite a big thing knowing the name and everything because all those years you think about it, and being a teacher too I used to think maybe I've taught the person. I had no idea that he was in Hong Kong. I could have known the person. I mean that always went through my mind, and at last knowing the name at least, and knowing that you could contact – I think that was quite important. That's probably why I haven't taken it any further because I know that I can now, whereas before I couldn't.

Since it is well established from bereavement research that availability of information about lost relatives can assist grieving, the mental health effects of getting some information were explored briefly in the present survey. Analyses were carried out of the psychological well-being, and recent feelings about adoption events, of sub-groups of pre-reunion mothers who had received anything from no information to identifying information about their relinquished child (see Table 2). The level of information available to mothers significantly influenced their GHQ-28 scores and self-esteem levels. Statistical comparison of the arithmetic means of the variables in Table 2 revealed that in each case birth mothers with no information had significantly poorer well-being scores than those with some non-identifying information. Lack of information was also associated with significantly more intense recent feelings of loss and guilt, with those having no information again feeling most negative. Thus, there was strong support from the survey for previous findings[8] that birth mothers' long-term psychological adjustment is facilitated by knowledge about the well-being of the child they relinquished.

Table 2

Means of psychological well-being and recent feelings variables for pre-reunion mothers who possessed different levels of information about their relinquished children

	Level of information available		
Variable*	None at all (n=45)	Non-identifying only (n=39)	Identifying (eg name) (n=65)
GHQ-28	52.74	45.32	47.26
Self-esteem	21.74	18.13	19.51
Loss feelings	3.93	3.26	3.50
Sadness feelings	3.83	3.29	3.55
Guilt feelings	3.33	2.11	2.95
Relief feelings	4.12	4.08	3.81
Calm feelings	4.30	3.78	3.83
Joy feelings	4.53	4.06	4.08

* *Higher scores indicate lower psychological well-being*

145

Feelings about the renewed contact

Not surprisingly, most birth mothers felt extremely nervous and uncertain just before the initial reunion, and many said that they experienced a mix of intense positive and negative emotions around the time of the reunion. The survey compared the mothers' recollection of their feelings about adoption events at the time of the initial reunion with their feelings in the most recent months. Their average ratings of affect at the time of the first reunion were more intensely positive for all six emotions (see Table 1) than at the present time, and significantly so for feelings of loss, relief and joy. These results indicate a moving down from the emotional volatility of the initial reunion to a period of more stable adjustment in its aftermath. A majority of the post-reunion women who were interviewed also indicated a sense of working through feelings or loss during the period after the initial re-contact.

When asked in the survey how satisfied overall they were with the renewed contact with their child, 61 per cent were 'totally' or 'very' satisfied, 23 per cent were 'moderately' satisfied, while only 16 per cent reported being 'not very' or 'not at all' satisfied. Although a majority of the mothers who had experienced renewed contact reported feeling at least 'very satisfied', 107 of them gave some reason for dissatisfaction with the new contact. In fact, there were marked individual differences in the comments mothers made after rating that they were 'totally' satisfied. For example, one mother, who first re-contacted her daughter two and a half years ago, said:

> I was very angry when the 'Bill' was being passed. I felt it an invasion of my privacy. When I met my child I felt nothing – she was just another young woman. My own daughter and her see each other regularly as they both live in Auckland and neither has another sister.

On the other hand, a more typical comment associated with a rating of 'total' satisfaction was:

> This reunion experience has been the most wonderful, 'special' feeling in my life. I now have a much more positive attitude with myself and life. (Mother who first re-contacted her son 25 months earlier.)

A content analysis of the reasons for dissatisfaction mentioned by the 107 post-reunion women yielded seven main causes for dissatisfaction

146

and the frequencies of these are shown in Table 3. Individual case examples of these categories of dissatisfaction are presented in Table 4. The most clear outcome of this analysis was that reasons 3, 4 and 5 were the most common and were often interrelated. One could say that the mothers who articulated their disappointments with re-contact most often complained of difficulty in developing a satis-fyingly close relationship and this was sometimes associated with physical impediments to closer contact such as distance or infrequency of communications.

It should be noted that only a small percentage of mothers said that negative attitudes of adoptive family members were a problem. This feeling was confirmed in the interview phase when eight mothers expressed the opinion that they did not want their relationship with the adopted child to hurt the adoptive parents or place a strain on existing relationships within the adoptive family. Eight mothers also expressed the feeling that the adoptive parents were the 'real parents' of their child.

Table 3

Main reason for dissatisfaction with renewed contact

		%	n
1	Negative attitude of adoptive parents or relatives of the adopted person	8.4	9
2	Negative aspects of the adopted person's behaviour other than delay in re-contact	17.8	19
3	Distance causing a problem with frequency of contact	20.6	22
4	Infrequent or delayed re-contact by adopted person after initial contact	22.4	24
5	Problems in achieving a satisfyingly close personal relationship with the adopted person	25.2	27
6	Regret about lost relationship or parenting opportunities	2.8	3
7	Other	2.8	3

Table 4

Examples of reasons for dissatisfaction with renewed contact

1   Negative attitude of adoptive parents or relatives of the adopted person.

> The main reason is her parents. She was not told she was adopted till the parents were approached by the Department of Social Welfare when she was 22½. They'd never intended to tell her. Due to their attitude she is unable to contact me freely and due to their wishes has continued to stay anonymous. We have now met three times and although these meetings have been wonderful, their uncompromising stand is palling the joy. She has the guilt of their secrecy now. (Mother, first contact 18 months earlier)

2   Negative aspects of the adopted person's behaviour other than delay in re-contact.

> My son is very loving towards me but he has a big chip on his shoulder about me giving him up, he lays a guilt trip on me often saying he wished I never gave him up as it would have been better for him to have been with me. It leaves me screwed up, wishing I could make it up to him and then sometimes regretting finding him, for many reasons. But I'm his mother. I love him. (Mother, first contact 15 months earlier when son was 21 years old)

3   Distance causing a problem with frequency of contact.

> Because he lives a distance away and is not able to visit often. I feel that it is very difficult to establish a relationship in any depth. It is frustrating – but I do accept the reality of the situation. it may change in the future. (Mother, first contact 23 months earlier when son was 26)

> Because we get on very well since our first contact I would love to see him all the time. However, because of work commitments he has had to move and consequently our contact is not as often now. At 22 years of age he is also trying to make a life and career for himself. It's natural for him but difficult for me after only finding him 18 months ago.

4   Infrequent or delayed re-contact by the adopted person after
    initial contact.

> I was thrilled when my son, whose adoptive mother had
> written in reply to my search for him, from Queensland,
> called into New Zealand to visit me en route from Hawaii to
> Queensland, but I have not heard from him since. I would
> love to hear. His mother has sent a Christmas card – I had
> already sent one to him. I am conscious of intruding into a
> family. (Mother, first contact 12 months earlier when son
> was 28 years old)

5   Problems in achieving a satisfyingly close personal relationship
    with the daughter or son.

> I'd like to have maintained a more regular contact . . . but . . . I
> feel that I mustn't encroach on his time too much for fear
> that this might drive him away although he's assured me that
> this would never happen. (Mother, first contact 20 months
> earlier when son was 20)

> I feel that we still need to have honest talks about our
> feelings towards each other, and the adoption triangle to
> reach the closeness that I wish for. But this is due to my own
> inability to express emotions that have been so severely
> repressed for 30 years that they now deny expression. I am
> still too shamed. (Mother, first contact 22 months earlier
> when daughter was 32)

6   Regret about lost relationship or parenting opportunities.

> I can never be a mother to my daughter to the same degree as
> I am to my younger daughter. Neither she nor I have the
> bonding we would have had, had she stayed with me. This is
> the reason for my sorrow. (Mother, first contact 19 months
> earlier, when daughter was 20)

7   Other reasons for dissatisfaction.

> Not enough help from Social Welfare, who put us in touch
> but that was all. (Mother, first contact six months earlier,
> when son was 22)

Views on current procedures

Mothers were questioned in the survey as to whether they received any 'counselling or support from either a self-help agency ... or a professional' before or after the initial reunion, and whether they felt 'adequately prepared for the event and its consequences'. A total of 47 per cent said they did not receive any counselling or support before the initial reunion, and 75 per cent said they did not get any such help after the reunion. Women who received some counselling before the reunion did report feeling significantly better prepared than those who had not received such help. However, the prior counselling did not result in significantly higher overall satisfaction with contact or less intense negative feelings immediately after initial contact. Mothers who raised the issue of counselling in their interviews had widely varying opinions on the usefulness of any counselling that they may have received. However, their views on the present procedures for getting adoption-related information were more consistent.

Birth mothers have less entitlement to information under the new Act than their adopted childen and they have less control over the search process. Mothers were asked: 'Do you think that the current procedures for trying to make contact ... should be changed in any way?' Those who stated a need for change argued that birth mothers' access to information should be more in line with that of their adopted sons or daughters. The interviewed mothers were also asked whether they thought it was best to keep the legislated age minimum of 20 years before re-contact could be attempted, and whether the veto powers of each party should be kept as they were. Table 5 shows the way the 21 interviewees responded to these questions. It is

Table 5

Distribution of opinions expressed by interviewees about the current legislative provisions on adopted person age minimum and vetoes (n=21)

	Depends on the individual	Remove or lower	Retain as is
Adopted person age minimum of ·20 years	8	6	7
Veto potential for each party	8	5	8

interesting to note that this small group of birth mothers, who had taken at least some action toward re-contact, appeared quite evenly split on the contentious issue of balancing rights of privacy and rights to know. One is left with an impression, also mentioned by others,[9] that a significant proportion of birth mothers tend to feel a lack of entitlement to equal rights with adult adopted persons. Thus, their behaviour can be a reflection of the power balance that they find themselves confronting in the present, as well as a result of past experiences.

Conclusions

In the case of birth mothers who have experienced closed adoptions, this study has once again shown the crucial importance of access to information about the relinquished child. Not only was a lack of information associated with predictably higher feelings of guilt, but mothers lacking information also had significantly lower levels of self-esteem and general psychological well-being. This finding confirms the mental health benefits of more recent open adoption practices in New Zealand and elsewhere. As Reich[10] has succinctly stated:

> Knowledge, leading to direct contact, at least in adulthood, reduces the risk of the void being filled by unhappiness, which can become a form of fidelity to the lost child. Living with uncertainty is one of the most anxiety provoking aspects of adoption for all three parties, but it can be minimised.

Another clear outcome of the present study is that a solid majority of birth mothers who applied for information and eventually made personal contact with relinquished children were very satisfied overall with that contact. This finding is backed up by archival analyses of 2000 birth mother applications by Preston,[11] who also found that over 80 per cent of adopted persons responded positively to an approach under the Act. The finding in this study, that the main source of dissatisfaction with re-contact related to difficulties in forming satisfyingly close relationships, may help to inform current counselling efforts with birth mothers planning to meet an adult daughter or son. The developmental tasks and needs facing young adults are often somewhat in conflict with the forming of such cross-generational relationships. Sensitivity to these different developmental stages is a necessary component of successful adjustment to reunion for all parties.

The last decade has seen a growth in social work and media attention to the past and present victimisation of birth mothers.[12] What now seems necessary is more practical help to birth mothers and adopted people to ensure that they retain their self-esteem and sense of control over their lives. The strains and uncertainties of renewed contact were apparent from the comments of many women in this research. What was even more striking, however, was the fact that in almost all cases, including those who did not like what they found, the reunion was seen from a psychological point of view as a positive growth experience.

Acknowledgements

I wish to acknowledge how grateful I am to the women who participated in this study and shared often painful memories with me. The work was stimulated and encouraged by Karen Svendsen and Chris Inglis of the Aotearoa Birthmothers Support group and by Ron Benjamin and Moya Shaw from the Adult Adoption Information Section in the Auckland Department of Social Welfare. The sample recruitment was made possible by the help of Bryony Walker, Ross MacKay and Clare Dominick of the research section of the Department of Social Welfare. The excellent help of Keith Macky on data entry and analysis is very much appreciated. I am grateful to Kris Fernando, Pam Clarke, Kathryn McPhillips and Heather Scott for their interviewing of birth mothers. Finally I would like to thank the Social Sciences Research Fund Committee for their financial support of this work.

References

1   Rockel J and Ryburn M *Adoption today: change and choice in New Zealand,* Auckland: Heinemann Reid, 1988.

2   Condon J T 'Psychological disability in women who relinquish a baby for adoption' *The Medical Journal of Australia* 144, 1986.
Shawyer J *Death by adoption* Auckland: Cicada Press, 1979.
Dominick C 'Early contact in adoption: contact between birth mothers and adoptive parents at the time of and after the adoption' Research Series no 10, Wellington: Department of Social Welfare, 1988.

3   Reich D 'Re-discovering birth mothers' *Adoption & Fostering* 14 3, 1990. See also 2 above.

4   Winkler R and van Keppel M 'Relinquishing mothers in adoption'
    Melbourne: Institute of Family Studies, 1984.

5   Langridge L 'Adoption: the birthmother's experience' Unpublished MA
    Thesis, University of Auckland, 1984.

6   See 2 and 4 above.

7   Preston E 'Adult Adoption Information Act 1985: An analysis of 2,000
    applications from birth parents under Section 8' Paper presented at the
    Adoption Conference, Wellington, May 1990.

8   See 2 and 4 above.

9   See 2 (Shawyer) and 7 above.

10 See 3 above.

11 See 7 above.

12 See 3 above.

11 Access to adoption records: the results of the changes in New Zealand law

Keith C. Griffith

The background

To recap the legal situation, the New Zealand Adult Adoption Information Act, 1985, provides that adult adopted people aged 20 years and over can obtain their original birth entry as of right. Counselling is provided. A birth parent of an adult adopted person may obtain the adoptive entry, subject to the adopted person's consent. A state agency conducts the search for the person whose consent is required. Either party may place a veto on the release of any identifying information concerning them. A veto lasts 10 years and is renewable.

Use of adoption information law

In, the period from 1 September 1986 to 31 August 1989, 10,676 adopted people in New Zealand applied for their birth entries. (This compares with an estimated 66,000 adopted people, of whom two-thirds were adopted by strangers.) Of those applying, 7196 were female and 3460 were male. The number of birth parents applying for information was 2464 and, not surprisingly, showed an even stronger bias towards female applicants with 2311 birth mothers and only 153 birth fathers using the legislation. The typical waiting time was about three weeks for adopted people and about three to four months for birth parents (because they have to wait for the adopted person to be contacted).

During the six-month lead-in to the legislation, from 1 March 1986, 3749 vetoes were placed. This was followed by only a further 430 over the next three years. Of the total number of vetoes, birth mothers placed 3041, birth fathers 63, and adopted people 1075. Approximately six per cent of applicants strike a veto. Despite having been introduced to give protection, in practice vetoes appear to make adopted people more determined to search and contact. About half manage to circumvent the veto by one means or another.

Surprisingly, despite doing so, many are received positively. Birth parents talk of having placed the veto out of fear, or as a result of hearing horror stories early on, but many say that they now know of successful contacts and are glad to have been contacted themselves. Other will have been afraid of their husband finding out but are reassured by a tactful and sensitive form of contact by the adopted person. They not untypically find that they have a lot in common with their son or daughter.

Approximately one in four adult adopted people in stranger adoptions applied for information in the first four years of the Act. (As yet unpublished work by Mary Iwanek of Victoria University, Wellington, indicates that in the period up to 1991 approximately 40 per cent of all adopted people who were adopted by strangers in New Zealand and who have now reached adulthood have obtained identifying information under the Act.) This compares with four per cent in England and Wales and six per cent in Israel. Possible reasons for the higher rate of applications in New Zealand include the ten-year campaign leading up to the change, which drew good media coverage and was accompanied by advertising of the legal changes, and an effective educational programme. The nature of New Zealand society itself may also have been a contributory factor. It is much less divided along class lines, for example, than is British society so perhaps people were less constrained from finding their roots. Also, once an idea takes off there, it tends to take firm hold. The objective of the campaigners had been not just law change, but altered public and professional attitudes to adoption. The new openness did indeed create a suitable climate for change.

Results of access to adoption information

Taking together the 10,676 adopted people who used the Act in the first three years, plus the 22,000 others who had had non-stranger adoptions, we arrive at a situation where almost half of adult adopted people in New Zealand now have identifying information about their birth origins.

Most adopted people seeking birth entry information go on to try and find out more and often to meet their birth parents. From a sample of adopted people contacting birth parents, 80 per cent received a positive response. The ratio of those who go on to form continuing relationships with birth parents or siblings, as against those who only exchange information, is in the region of five to three. Of the remaining 20 per cent of the total who seek a reunion, half are greeted with an equivocal reply such as 'I don't know if I want to

155

know you', and the other half face a rejection. Of these last, however, some try again a year or two later and about half of them meet with success on the second occasion.

Most families in New Zealand, in a population of under four million, now know of reunions in their kin or community. Positive results have been a stimulus to change. Social change was required to gain sufficient support for the legislative reform. Since then, the process has become self-perpetuating with the changes implemented by the legislation itself having helped to create further social change. The appearance of a wide range of responsible adopted people, birth parents and adoptive parents in the media, following reunions, gave credence to the adoption law change. It gave members of the adoption triad new confidence to speak out and not be ashamed of their status. The debate on openness created new openness. For decades, a cloak of secrecy hung over adoption, concealing facts and frustrating research. Agency-dominated theory and practice reigned supreme, thwarting and discouraging examination of its true effects. The law change has enabled people to tell their stories. Old myths are dying and a new and deeper understanding of adoption has come into being.

Responses of adoptive parents
In submissions preceding the passing of the 1985 Act, adoptive parents were equally divided. Half supported the change in the law and half were opposed. Since then, there has been an increasingly positive response from adoptive parents.

Extensive media coverage of the changes, and of a range of related issues, has made adoption an open topic for public discussion. At the same time, it has also opened up discussion in adoptive families, since cover-ups are no longer an option. The truth has to be faced. The adopted person, once an adult, can contact or be contacted by a birth parent. Stories about birth parents can be checked out. They are no longer shadowy people, cut off for ever, but real people who one day may turn up in real life. Many adoptive parents feared they might lose their child. However, where parents have encouraged their adopted son or daughter in their search, it has almost invariably strengthened family ties. This has been a most commonly reported benefit of reunions.

Now, more adoptive parents of younger children are seeking contact with birth mothers. After all, if you are going to be able to meet at 20, why not meet earlier if mutually agreed? For those under 20, access through the courts on special grounds appears to have had good success with teenagers, helping them resolve self-identity issues.

Responses of adopted people

Most adopted people who search are normal, well-adjusted adults. Theirs is fundamentally a search for personal truth, integrity and social identity. The old, pathological models of searching have been found to apply only to a minority. Adopted people need to make their own decisions whether and when to search; it must be their choice. Some are not interested. For others it is an all-out quest; still others start and stop several times. It takes time to integrate new knowledge. Adopted people should neither be pushed into, nor thwarted in, their search for origins.

While adopted people seek to model themselves on the only parents they know, they cannot obliterate the reality of the other set of parents. To do so would be to do violence to reason, honesty and themselves. Adopted people have two sets of parents. Their birth parents gave them life and all their genetic make-up. Their adoptive parents have given them all their nurturing. Reunions have enabled the members of the adoption triad to accept each other. For some, the task is not easy. In my experience, however, when an adopted person is accepted by two sets of parents, they feel much more a whole person.

In my experience of meeting many hundreds of adoption 'consumers' around the world, adopted people conceived by rape or incest do not normally fall apart when they find out, as many professionals fear. They often cope much better than the people who try to help them. Adopted people have a basic coping method when they discover they were conceived in immoral or questionable ways. They say to themselves: 'If my birth parents had not done what they did, I would not be here! So I had better face reality. To fully accept myself, I must accept my origins.'

There is a basic element of rejection in any adoption. The adopted person has not been brought up by his or her birth parents. Some adopted people are more sensitive because of this, mopping up and re-interpreting everything that can be made to look like rejection. Some even set themselves up: 'If you won't reject me, I will make you.' Some completely reject the lifestyle of their adoptive families. This may be a radical search to find their own identity – and as such may not be dissimilar from the behaviour of some non-adopted young people – but sometimes it is done to provoke rejection. My reading and experience suggests that perhaps a fifth of adoptions fail to achieve complete success, and the child may be a misfit in the family. As teenagers, they may leave home, and cut themselves off from the adoptive family But, alas, an almost comparable number of children in non-adoptive families appear to suffer the same fate. Adoption is often blamed for the adopted person's problems, but in some cases causation may have little to do with adoption. Adoption is, however, an added stress factor.

Birth parents' responses

New Zealand was one of the first countries to give birth parents access to adoption information. The reform movement included many birth mothers and, backed by adopted people, they insisted that the days of secrecy and unresolved grief must come to an end. The women's movement also made a valued and continuing contribution to adoption law reform.

Birth parents can now be seen as real people. When the 'clean break' was practised, they had often been shadows whom, it was felt, the adopted person should never be allowed to know. At last, they are acknowledged as existing, and adult adopted people obtain information about them, can contact them, and establish a relationship with them.

The idea that birth mothers want to forget about their offspring and get on with their lives in anonymity seems largely to be a cruel myth perpetrated by adoption agencies. Most think a lot about their relinquished child. Most suffer from unresolved grief that continues throughout their life. Reunions help many birth mothers to resolve that grief. Birth fathers, too, are speaking out in increasing numbers. They can no longer be arbitrarily dismissed from adoption proceedings and decisions. They seek clarification of their place and their rights. Many birth fathers have a deep concern for their child, and some suffer grief at the loss of the child. In many reunions, birth fathers have taken an important and constructive role.

The issue of environment versus genetics

We have listened to hundreds of adopted people and birth parents telling of their reunions, we have heard them speak not only of discovering strong physical traits in common, but of having been surprised to find marked personality traits also. 'Not only does she look like me, she talks and thinks like me!' How people react under stress, their thinking processes, sense of humour, temper reactions, odd body movements, postures and gestures – in fact, much of what we regard as making up a personality appears to have strong genetic links.

The overwhelming belief that environment could overcome genetic endowment was a foundation of complete break theory and practice in adoption, and a justification for secrecy. There was, however, a lack of clear evidence; it is notoriously difficult to separate genetic from environmental influences. Adoption reunions can now cast new light on an old debate.

Speaking to adoptive parents, it seems that they found the environmentalism theory was comforting. A child brought up in their family environment could be expected to adopt their own traits. In reality, however, the child could be more difficult. Some manifested personalities adoptive families had never encountered before. A quiet, unemotional family might find itself confronted with a hot-blooded, quick-tempered, highly emotional child. Not only was the adopted person's emotional pattern quite different from the parents', but their thinking might also be unfamiliar, to the frustration of both parents and child. Many adoptive parents blamed themselves for not understanding the child. Likewise, the child found that he or she could not understand the parents and became unhappy and confused. Both the confusion and the search for someone to blame are eased by the recognition that genetic inheritance plays a greater role than previously allowed for.

Genetic traits continue to appear and develop throughout our lives. Some become evident in the early teenage years. Part of the task of finding and acknowledging our identity is owning and coming to terms with our genetic make-up, and this forms a key part of the adopted person's quest to discover him- or herself. Consequently, genetic aspects of personality have important implications for counselling. The genetic make-up of a person is more important than previously thought. It is more difficult counselling adopted people who are cut off from their genetic background because so much is unknown both to them and the counsellor. They are working in the dark. Attempts by the adopted person to change their basic personality can certainly create difficulties. Rather, what is needed is to endeavour to find the self in order to be true to oneself. At its worst, it is possible that some confused mental conditions may have a causation in genetic personality confusion, compounded by adoption by strangers under a model of secrecy.

With renewed interest in racial issues, genetic identity has assumed new importance. Western beliefs in the overwhelming influence of environment, and the consequent development of clean break adoption, have never been shared by most non-Western cultures. Adoption has become caught up in the issue of racial identity. Indeed, adoption itself has been brought into question. Should children ever be adopted outside their cultural or racial origins? This is a complex and pressing matter in which the needs of the child must remain paramount.

The replacement of the complete break and secrecy model by greater openness has brought into question whether there should be closed adoptions at all. A case is being made in New Zealand for adoption to be replaced by some form of protected guardianship. This could abolish the legal fiction involved in adoption.

Conclusion
Adoption information law change in New Zealand has not been a panacea for adoption problems. It has, however, made a major contribution to understanding adoption and alleviating some of the difficulties. It has also paved the way for further research and reform. Some of the key benefits of opening up birth and adoptive records to adopted people and their birth parents have been that it has:

- revealed the truth: we now know what happens to those personally involved, to the 'consumers' of adoption

- exposed much myth and ignorance

- increased accountability

- provided a wealth of real evidence for research and understanding

- reduced agency and social worker power

- enabled adopted people to find their full identity and to speak out

- helped deal with grief factors for all the parties in adoption

- allowed adoptive parents to see that they are not wholly responsible for their child's behaviour

- shown that both genetics and environment play an important role

- accelerated moves towards open adoption.

As openness increases for adult adopted people, more adoptive and birth parents in New Zealand are choosing open adoptive placements from the start. Birth mothers find that it eases their grief and that first-hand, up-to-date information about their child reduces anxiety. Open adoption is a subject which reveals deeply held but rarely expressed beliefs about the nature of parenthood, parental rights, 'ownership' of children, and sexual morality. Open adoption itself is neither easy nor problem-free. It can initially be more difficult – so many issues must be faced from the start – but, in the long term, this is all to the good. The adopted child's questions about the birth parents are easily answered: 'Ask her the next time we meet.' Indeed, accurate information is readily available to all the parties. For the adopters, entitlement is a little easier, espeically when the birth mother has chosen them and openly given her child to them, rather than the child being given to them by the agency. The adopted child, in turn, is able to incorporate both sets of parents into his or her own identity. As this happens naturally for a new generation of children, the heated debates over adult adoption information and reunions which preceded the legislative reform will increasingly become a part of history.

British Agencies for Adoption & Fostering

British Agencies for Adoption & Fostering (BAAF) is a registered charity and professional association for all those working in the child care field. BAAF's work includes:

providing training and consultation services to social workers and other professionals to help them improve the quality of medical, legal and social work services to children and families;

giving evidence to government committees on subjects concerning children and families;

responding to consultative documents on changes in legislation and regulations affecting children in or at risk of coming into care;

publishing a wide range of books, training packs, and leaflets as well as a quarterly journal on adoption, fostering and child care issues;

giving advice and information to members of the public on aspects of adoption, fostering and child care issues;

and helping to find new families for children through the BAAF Exchange Service, 'Be My Parent', and 'Find a Family'.

More information about BAAF (including membership subscription details) can be obtained from BAAF, 11 Southwark Street, London SE1 1RQ.